CHANGING TIMES

by

John Parsons

Best wishes

John Parsons. 11/3/06 .

'CHANGING TIMES'

Published in 2006 by **Beanshoots**

First Edition 2006, edited and published by Beanshoots.
Printed and bound by Wessex Malthouse Direct, Taunton.

Published by **Beanshoots**
Deer Holt, Ellicombe, TA24 6TT
01643 703597

ISBN 0-9551693-1-3

CONTENTS

PREFACE

My first book, 'Good Times - Bad Times', told the story of Cuthbert, known to everyone as Jon Hawkes, from the time he was born, until he died in 1924 aged 76.

I was often asked what happened to the family after their grandfather died. To provide the answer I have written 'Changing Times' as a sequel.

This is the story of Jon's grandson, William, born in 1909 and his granddaughter, Mary-Ann, born in 1911. It is also the story of their mother, Mary, after their father Bill, Jon's son, was killed in the Great War in 1917.

Many of the events described in this book occurred and the locations may be recognised by those that know the area. Similarly, some of the characters appearing in the book were actual people, whose part in the rich tapestry of West Somerset life is acknowledged. All other characters are fictitious.

A glossary is given at the end of the book for those words which may be unfamiliar to the modern reader. They are indicated in the text with an asterisk *.

EARLY DAYS

For William, growing up in Somerset during the years before the Great War, every day during the Spring and Summer months seemed to be warm and sunny, and to be remembered for many years afterwards. The cold, wet, and snowy days of Autumn and Winter were soon forgotten.

Shortly after he had learned to walk, William could often be seen on his father's baker's van, strapped in a child's harness attached to a hook behind the driver's seat to ensure that he could not fall off the van, as father and son made their way around the village, delivering bread.

On Sunday mornings when the horse was being groomed, and the horse brasses polished, William would be seen running around the yard, dodging the grown-ups, and diving between the legs of the horse which, like all the horses that Bill worked with, was called Tom. The horse seemed to realise that under no circumstances was he allowed to nip or kick the small boy, no matter how many times the wee lad was around his feet. All other human beings were fair game, if he was in that sort of mood. The horse towered above William and the sight of the horse gently lowering his head to take the odd cake or handful of oats from young William's hand, always brought an "aaaaah" from any onlookers.

After his sister was born and had grown up a little, they would both be taken for walks by their dad in the Quantock Hills, and if their mum came too, they would often take a picnic. The family would sometimes bring back wild flowers or lavender for the house, depending on the time of the year.

After William started school, he would wander down to the station in the evenings and on Saturdays, or during the school holidays, to see his grandpa. If the stationmaster was around, William knew better than to march down the platform and up the stairs into the signal box. Instead he would stand on tiptoe to peer over the parapet of the road bridge that crossed the railway line at the north end of the platform, until Mr Morris was out of sight.

When the stationmaster was not around, William would often accompany his grandpa down the platform to hand over the 'staff' to the loco crew of the train going in the 'down' direction, in the hope that, as the staff was handed over by his grandpa to the footplate crew, the engine driver would ask if the 'sprog' (William) would like a trip on the footplate. In a flash William would be up the step and into the cab, quickly taking his place below the edge of the cab side sheet, and only peering over the top of the cut-out to see the large coupling rods going up and down, when the train was out of the station limits.

He was usually taken on the engine for a trip to Crowcombe, or if he was very lucky, to Williton. At the end of his journey the driver would bring his engine to a stand, opposite the cab of the loco going in the other direction, and young William would be passed across the gap between the locomotives to the other crew, with instructions that the 'sprog' was to be handed over to the 'Bobby' (signalman) at Bishops Lydeard.

At first William was puzzled why all his journeys were to either Crowcombe or Williton, but he soon discovered that 'THEY' (the Management) were often at Norton Fitzwarren on the main line, and Management did not share the same enlightened view about small boys travelling on the footplates of their engines, as did the operating staff.

William was only eight years old when the sad news of his father's death at the front was received – too young to fully understand the implications of the news. Later, he began to realise that his father would not be coming home. There would be no more playing football on the recreation ground or family walks in the Quantocks. Even Tom, the baker's horse, seemed to sense that never again would Bill be coming to groom him on a Sunday morning.

When William was informed by his grandma, Amy, that he was now 'the man of the house', he took his responsibilities very seriously, and tried to do many of the tasks that his father had done, to help his mother. Mary was still working full-time in the bakery and she would often find William struggling to bring in the full coal scuttle, cleaning the hearth, or lighting the fire in the morning while she checked that there were no problems in the bake-house, that all the staff were present, and everything was ready for the start of the day.

The next hard lesson in life that William had to learn, was in 1918 when he attended his grandma Amy's funeral at St Mary's church, with his grandpa, mother and sister. Following the death of her only son his grandma no longer seemed to have time to laugh, and play with the two children, as she had done in the past. Although she was very fit for her age, to those that knew her well she appeared to have lost all her zest for life, and she had died and was buried within a fortnight of catching influenza. As far back as he could remember William had been told that, "big boys don't cry," and after his father's death young William had tried hard to conceal just how miserable and unhappy he really was.

The sight of his grandpa, who as far as William was aware had never shown any signs of emotion before, weeping in the Church and at the graveside, as he grieved over the loss of his Amy, made William realise that it was no disgrace to feel sad. Still unable to show his emotions in public William rushed home ahead of his mother as soon as the service had finished, dashed straight up to his bedroom, slammed the door and cried until he could cry no more.

Mary-Ann went back with her grandpa to his house to help him make his tea, and when Mary returned to her flat above the bakery she could hear William sobbing in his bedroom. Her first instinct was to rush into his room to comfort him, but realising that her son was unable to hide his grief any longer, she decided to let him cry for a short while, until eventually she could no longer bear to hear his sobs and went in to comfort him.

Because of his increased responsibilities, William's visits to his Grandpa's signal box became less frequent, although his interest in Railways remained undiminished.

After his mother had lost her job at the bakery (see 'Good Times - Bad Times', chapter 'Bad Times') and all three of them moved into their grandpa's house, William pestered his Nanny Annie (Mary's Mother), who was still running the Post Office and newsagent's shop, to allow him to do a paper round, so that he could contribute his wages of two shillings and sixpence (12.5p) towards the family finances.

After his grandpa had officially retired from the Railway, and had moved into the crossing keeper's cottage at Roebuck Lane crossing, William's visits to the signal box ceased altogether, which was probably just as well as the man who took his grandpa's place, a Mr Martin, had spent four years in the Army and before that many years in the service of the Great Western Railway. The notice on the door of the signal box read:

GREAT WESTERN RAILWAY
NOTICE
NO UNAUTHORISED PERSON ALLOWED IN THIS BOX
BY ORDER

---

and orders were meant to be obeyed at all times. This ruling applied especially to small boys.

Although he could not prevent his inspector Mr Harris, or the stationmaster Mr Morris, or even his relief signalman from entering 'his' box, Mr Martin insisted that anyone else who entered stepped onto two felt pads, and then shuffled their way around the floor of the box at all times. This was to ensure that the highly polished floor was not marked in any way. Drivers or Firemen who had to report to the signalmen for any reason stood no chance of gaining entry to the signal box even if it was pouring with rain. They therefore had to shout their message through the open door. If the register needed to be signed by the Driver or the Fireman the register was brought to the porch outside the door of the signal box to be signed.

It was no surprise to anyone at the Station except Mr Martin, that once the coal allowance for his signal box had been used, when he placed the coal scuttle on the platform alongside the cab of a passing engine it remained empty.

These problems did not prevent young William from wandering down to the station whenever he wanted to visit his grandpa at his crossing keeper's cottage. He would stand on the steps leading from the road to the down platform, and when any of the drivers who knew him waved for him to join them, he would run down the steps and jump up into the loco cab as soon as Mr Martin's back was turned. They would then bring their train to a standstill at the crossing, at the same time informing the keeper that they had a visitor for him. During one of these visits, as his grandpa was opening the level crossing gates William told him of Mr Martin's obsession with the polishing pads, causing his grandpa to laugh so much that he was almost hit by a large lump of coal that 'accidentally' fell from the passing loco.

His sister could not be persuaded to travel on the dirty footplate with her brother, and if she wished to visit her grandpa she always purchased a ticket to Crowcombe Station and travelled in the train

After alighting at the station she would walk along the line to her grandpa's cottage. As the reader will gather from the foregoing remarks, although both the children were similar in appearance, temperamentally they were poles apart. When she was a baby Mary-Ann would spend many hours in her cot underneath the counter in the baker's shop where her mother could keep an eye on her. Apart from the occasional gurgling noise coming from underneath the counter many of the customers in the shop were completely unaware that she was even there.

As she grew up she would spend many hours watching the lumps of dough come rolling down the wooden ramp from the floor above, for the bakers to knead and then place in tins, before they were put in the oven to bake. At other times she could be found watching her mother as she went about her many tasks, and before long would be trying to help with the washing up, or the cooking. To help them pass the time in the evenings, Mary taught her daughter how to knit, embroider, crochet, and even cut wool to make woollen slip mats. These were placed on the floor alongside the bed to ease the shock of putting their feet onto cold linoleum when they got out of bed in the morning. Mary was surprised how quickly the child learned quite complex tasks, and before long, apart from making slip mats, she was crocheting anti-macassars* for the chairs, and even embroidering tablecloths. Impressed as Mary was with her daughter's dexterity she was even more surprised at her mental agility.

When there were no customers in the shop, Mary would spend time reading to her daughter and by the time Mary-Ann started school she was able to read, having progressed from comics like 'Chick's Own' to 'Alice in Wonderland'. When the lending library opened in the Village Mary-Ann was a frequent visitor, and by the time she was eight years old had read 'Gulliver's Travels' and many of the books by Charles Dickens. Shortly after she had started school she had learned her times tables. Her spelling and writing standards had already passed those of her brother who had been at the school two years longer than his sister.

William was a plodder, like his father and grandfather before him. He soon became fed up when he was wrestling with a sum, or trying to work out whether a certain word should be spelt there, or their; he was reminded by the teacher that his sister had not found any problem with that work. When the children arrived home in the evening Mary-Ann tried to help her brother by giving him extra lessons, but soon gave him up as a lost cause from an educational point of view.

Mary had quickly recovered from the shock of being dismissed from the bakery in 1919, and as soon as the family had settled in her father-in-law's house, she set about the task of finding herself a job. She found that there were no suitable jobs in the village, but there was a vacancy for a book-keeper in the shirt factory in Viney Street, Taunton. After she had applied in writing for the post, and had been invited to attend an interview, she was more than a little upset when, during the course of the interview, she was informed that in spite of her experience they would prefer a man for the post. It was at this point she decided that she had better continue to look for other work.

On the Monday of the following week, just as she was getting the washing out of the copper*, she was startled by someone hammering frantically on the front door. Red-faced because of all the steam in the kitchen, she opened the front door and she saw that it was the telegraph boy. He promptly thrust an envelope in her hand, and having obtained her signature, jumped on his bike and without another word, pedalled back down the street as fast as he could. In the past, because telegrams had always brought her bad news of which she had received plenty recently, she assumed that it was more of the same. She took some time before she could summon up the courage to open the envelope with trembling hands, and was surprised to read that the Manager of the shirt factory had decided to offer her the job as a book-keeper, and that a confirmation letter would follow. When the letter arrived the following day, outlining the terms of her employment, the writer observed that he hoped that she would find the terms satisfactory, and unless she informed him to the contrary, he would assume that she would be able to start work with the company on the following Monday.

Although she knew that she would have to pay her fares into Taunton, the wages she had been offered were nearly twice as much as she had been receiving at the bakery, and she thought that her recent struggles to make ends meet might at last be coming to an end.

Still trembling, and at the same time dazed and excited at the change in her fortunes, she tried to put the clothes and sheets she had just washed through the mangle*, before hanging them out on the clothes line. In her excitement she failed to fold the newly washed items properly, with the result that the wringer often jammed as she tried to turn the handle and she had to reverse the items out from the rollers, refold them and put them through the wringer again. When the shirts did go through the rollers they managed to break most of the buttons; which meant more work for Mary later when she had to sew on new buttons. Because it took her so much longer to do the washing that morning, the evening meal for the family was rather late as the spotted dick they had always eaten on Mondays could not be boiled in the copper until the washing had been finished. The meal was further delayed as Mary had to give each member of the family her good news immediately they came through the door.

Because the meal was so late, after she had finished the washing up, with Mary-Ann's help, when Mary came to heat up the flat irons on the range, to iron the clothes she had washed, she found that the fire in the grate was so low she could not do her ironing until the following morning. Although they did not realise it then, that would be the last time they were to have Spotted Dick on a Monday; in future, washing day would be on a Saturday.

A NEW JOB

When Mary arrived at the shirt factory in Viney Street on the following Monday morning she was shown into a small office. On the left of the door she had entered were two long narrow windows, and beneath each window was a Victorian oak pedestal desk. The tops were covered in green leather, which was badly marked after many years of service. On each desk there was a glass ink stand with two inkwells, one for red ink, the other for black, and a selection of wooden-handled pens with steel nibs. On each desk there was also a wooden ruler, blotter, and blotting pad, and by each desk a hard wooden chair, only one of which had arm rests.

Against the opposite wall an enormous five foot high safe stood on the floor, and next to the safe was a door leading into another office, which Mary was later to learn was the Cashier's office. Against the wall behind the desks there was a number of wooden shelves containing numerous box files labelled, 'advice notes'; 'remittance advice notes'; 'statements'; 'copy invoices', etc., together with the start and finish dates of their contents. Other shelves contained ledgers, bound in green leatherette with red spine covers containing the legend, 'Sales ledger' or 'Bought ledger' in gold leaf on the spine.

The only other furniture in the room was a free-standing wooden coat, hat, and umbrella stand, which held a well-worn bowler hat, and a furled umbrella in the drip tray at the bottom of the stand. Mary observed that the whole room was lit by a single electric light bulb in the middle of the high ceiling, and she wondered how on earth they were expected to be able to see to work in the office, when the dark evenings of Winter arrived. She was later to find out that in the Winter paraffin lamps were placed on each desk about two minutes before lighting up time.

She waited with the commissionaire who had brought her from the reception area, while the person who occupied the desk nearest the door slowly completed the entry he was making in the ledger in front of him. Although he was aware of their presence he ignored both completely for as long as he could. While Mary waited she noted that every personal item on his desk – pencils, pens, rubber, etc. – had his name, A. B. Leader, printed on them, and as she waited she idly wondered why he had marked everything on his desk in this way. Eventually he looked up, and the commissionaire introduced Mary to her new boss; having done so he turned and left the office.

Mr Leader, without bothering to look at her, or shake hands, then spoke to Mary, without rising from his seat.

"Your desk is over there. I suppose you know what you are supposed to do? All the work that has to be done is in the top right-hand drawer of your desk." As Mary went to sit at her desk she heard him mutter that he thought that a woman's place was in the home or on the factory floor, not in an office.

It was at this point that Mary realised why he used both initials: she decided that A Leader he was not, but a A. B. Leader he definitely was, but she found herself blushing every time the thought crossed her mind.

The charming Mr Leader was an elderly gentleman of approximately sixty years, about five feet six inches tall, rather rotund, white hair going a little thin on top, with a large walrus moustache which varied in colour from white, to brown, to dark brown, and back to brown, and then white along its length. He wore a blue striped suit, a white shirt and a white starched wing collar and blue tie. She was later to learn that, with the exception of his collar which he changed daily, and his socks and shirt which he changed weekly, he wore the same suit throughout the year, Summer and Winter. His only concession to the seasons was the thick woollen overcoat he wore during the winter. She had already realised that he was a snuff taker from the amount of snuff that had finished up down his tie, or in the folds of his waistcoat where it had ridden up over his stomach, but she was not prepared for the explosion that occurred a few minutes after she had started work, following his first snuff taking session after her arrival.

Not only did the windows rattle but she was so startled that many of the papers she had been sorting into order finished up on the floor, and she had to start sorting them all over again. Aware that in future similar disturbances were likely to occur on a regular basis because of his habit, she attempted to be prepared for these disturbances, but if she was concentrating on her work she would sometimes be caught unawares. If she was writing at the time it often caused her to jump and drop her pen, which would result in a crossed pen nib, which had to be replaced. As she was not allowed to keep any spare stationery herself, the request for a replacement had to be made to Mr Leader who would rummage in the top left hand drawer of his desk, and when he eventually found one would hold it out for her to come over to his desk and collect, at the same time muttering that he could not understand how she managed to break so many nibs, and would she please try to ensure that in future she made her nibs last as long as he did, because, "nibs cost money you know."

The other matter that concerned Mary when she first opened the Purchase Ledger for which she was responsible, was the number of differing types of handwriting that appeared on each sheet over the past few months. It was an observation which did not fill Mary with much confidence about her long term prospects with the company. Apart from the time when he was grumbling, Mr Leader made no other attempt at conversation and it was not very long before she realised that if she did say anything, she would simply be ignored.

She very quickly learned the procedures even without any help from Mr Leader but after she had been there about three months Mr Leader was called into the next office, and she could hear the level of the conversation gradually start to rise until Mr Leader, and Mr Forbes the cashier, were shouting at each other. Finally she heard Mr Leader shout, "That damn woman has made another mistake," before he came storming out of the office to address Mary

"You're in trouble now: Mr Forbes wishes to speak to you immediately." His tone of voice added meaning to his words.

Expecting to be dismissed immediately she knocked on the door of the Cashier's office, and was told to enter. She was surprised when Mr Forbes very quietly asked her, "Please sit down." He then explained the situation.

"One of our company's suppliers has refused to make any further deliveries of thread as their outstanding account has not been settled. Would you please look into the matter immediately and let me know what has happened?"

"Of course," she replied, already thinking through what may have happened.

Returning to her own office she quickly located the original advice note for the goods in question, together with the relevant invoice, and the copy of the remittance advice note that had been attached to the remainder of the paperwork, and had then been filed after the cheque had been sent. Finally, she checked in the post book and found that the cheque had been raised and sent out with the remittance advice note on the same day. Armed with all this information she returned to Mr Forbes and gave him all the facts, together with the appropriate paperwork to study.

After a while Mary was asked by Mr Forbes, "What do you think has happened?"

"I would think that either the letter has gone astray in the post, which is unlikely, or that a mistake has occurred in the offices of our supplier."

"Thank you. Please leave the paperwork with me so that I can write to the supplier. I will return all the documents to you shortly." As she was leaving the office Mr Forbes added, "Mary, could you inform Mr Leader that I would like to see him immediately."

"Of course," replied Mary, glad to return to her desk, passing on the message as she did so.

As Mr Leader went into the office, Mr Thompson, the other occupant of the office, was sent out, firmly shutting the door behind him. As he passed through her office he winked at Mary and whispered to her, "Well done!" This small act of kindness improved Mary's morale enormously, because at last she started to feel that she was not all alone.

She never did find out what had been said between the two men behind the closed door, but whatever it was it did nothing to improve Mr Leader's temper, nor did she receive any form of apology from him.

At dinner time (now called lunch time) that day Mr Thompson succeeded in upsetting Mr Leader still further when he informed Mary that he was going down to the 'pie and mash' shop along the road, and would she care to join him for something to eat. Although Mary was not hungry she quickly accepted his offer, welcoming the chance to get away from the glowering Mr Leader for just a few minutes.

During their thirty minute break Mr Thompson, or David as he asked her to call him, told her a little about himself.

"I don't wish to embarrass, or 'compromise' you by spending this break with you, but just to leave the office for a

16

while helps. I had worked for Mr Leader for four years before joining the forces, and if I had to choose again between Mr Leader and the trenches, I would prefer to do another four years in the trenches!" He then went on, "I decided that I would not return to my old job when I left the Army and it was only when I was assured that I would not have to work with Mr Leader again that I agreed to return to the Company. I know just how unpredictable our Mr Leader can be, especially when he is in the wrong. That's why I asked you to accompany me to get something to eat."

After that first time they often went out together during their mid-day break. After Mary had endured Mr Leader in one of his more belligerent moods all morning she found that just talking to David would soon have them laughing over matters, that only moments before had made her feel almost suicidal. She found him very easy to talk to, and he in turn found himself explaining why he had not married (a 'Dear John' letter received when he was still in the trenches) and why he had, until he met Mary, found it so difficult to relax in the company of women.

Perhaps not the most attractive man on the planet, he was about five feet eight inches tall, rather plump, clean shaven with his black brilliantined* hair already starting to go grey at the temples, combed straight back. He walked with a slight limp as a result of a bullet wound in his calf. She liked the rather charming, slightly old fashioned way that he behaved when they were together, by opening doors for her, standing up when she came into a room, moving her chair for her when she was leaving a table, and insisting that he walked on the outside of the pavement as they went down the road. But he could not flatter her, so that she felt so special, bring her small treats, or make her laugh even in adversity, in the way her Bill had always done

Although she did not realise it at the time the events of that day, when she first lunched with David, were to have a profound effect on the remainder of her life.

CHANGING TIMES

The year 1922 was to turn out to be the year that Mary had to make a number of decisions that were to affect not only her own life, but the lives of her family and others that she knew.

After the never-to-be-forgotten altercation between Mr Leader and Mr Forbes, Mary continued to meet David outside the office. At first David simply walked with her to the station in the evenings, and after she had entered the station, he then walked back to his parents' house in Belvedere Road, which was only a short distance away. After a time, although nothing was said, Mary thought she noticed a slight change in his attitude towards her. Sometimes when they arrived at the station, he would purchase a penny platform ticket and see her onto the train, which was usually standing in the Bay Platform (Platform 6) and he would then stand talking to her through the open window of the carriage, until the train left at 6.35pm. He then left the station to continue his journey home.

Later he would sometimes accompany her on the train, and then walk with her to her home. Mary then felt that she had to invite him in for something to eat, and after sharing their evening meal, he would stay talking to them, often delaying his departure for so long before leaving to catch the last train, that he had only five minutes to cover the half mile to the station before the train left for Taunton at twelve minutes past eleven. He frequently had to run all the way down the road to catch the train, often arriving at the top of the driveway leading down to the station platform as the train was approaching under the road bridge, and drawing to a halt by the platform. Often he would still be only halfway down the driveway.

If the Guard was ready to depart, the ticket collector would call out to him that another passenger was coming. As David arrived at the ticket barrier he would be waved through, so that he would run up the platform passing the Guard, who would be standing tapping his foot, and glancing at his pocket watch and then dive into the first available compartment. As he closed the carriage door the Guard would flash his green light to the footplate crew, and as the train started to pull away from the station, would swing through the open door of his compartment, in the nonchalant manner that all GWR* Guards managed to achieve.

On Saturdays, after leaving work at midday they would meet in Taunton and either go shopping, or more often window shopping, together. Occasionally they would go to the 'pictures' (cinema), or back to his parents' house, leaving in good time for Mary to get to the station in time for her to catch the last train back to Bishops Lydeard at 8.15pm.

On Sundays, there were no opportunities for them to meet, because no trains ran to Minehead on the Lord's Day. Mary tried to catch up with her housework or the washing that she had not been able to do during the week, even though she realised that she could not hang it out on the line on a Sunday, without upsetting the neighbours. She always hoped that it would stay fine on Monday so that she could get it dry. At the same time she would be cooking the traditional Sunday roast dinner for the children and her father-in-law, who always came over on a Sunday, so that he could keep in touch with all their news. David attended morning and evening services at the local Baptist Church in Taunton, and he also taught at the Sunday school.

One night, David left Mary's house even later than usual to catch the last train, and when he arrived on the platform, saw the train pulling out of the station. After running three quarters of the length of the platform after the rapidly accelerating train, the Guard finally saw him and, 'put in the setter' (applied the emergency brake) bringing the train to a halt just before the guard's van cleared the end of the platform, enabling David to travel in the Guard's van to Taunton instead of walking. After David had scrambled aboard, and the guard had got the train underway again, he turned to David and said, "Nearly missed the train that time, Sir!"

A few days after this escapade, David informed Mary that he had decided to set up house on his own, and that he had found a house in Minehead Road at the bottom of her village; would she mind if he moved into the house? Although she was worried what time he would leave her house when he visited her in the evenings, without the restraint of catching the last train, she felt that she could hardly say she objected. After he had obtained the major items he needed, Mary helped him sort out the many small items required to completely furnish the new house. Mary had also sewn the curtains that he needed. To say thank you for the kindness Mary had shown him, David invited her and the children, together with her father-in-law, to Sunday lunch, and it was Mary's turn to be surprised at how competent a cook he really was.

Although there was no Baptist Church in the village, David soon became involved with the local Congregational Chapel, and Mary had Sundays to herself and the family. The only unfortunate consequence of David's invitation for her family to join him for Sunday lunch, was that her father-in-law became aware of David's presence in the Village, and he lost no time in asking Mary, "Who is that fellow?" Her explanation that, "He's just a man I work with," did not seem to convince him. Jon's suspicions were not banished when he heard that Mary was meeting David in Gore Square each morning, and walking down to the station with him to catch the train. Although he never said anything to Mary, Jon wondered if Mary would be as happy with David, as she had been with his Bill.

As the weeks went by, Mary became increasingly worried about the impact David's presence would have on the family. Although they were still good friends, she was worried what the reaction of her children would be if David did pluck up enough courage to ask her to marry him. What would she say to his proposal? What would be the reaction of Mary-Ann? Or William? Or even her father-in-law?

There was only one way to find out, and one evening when she was alone with Mary-Ann in the house she spoke to her about the problem, and was relieved to learn that her daughter rather liked David. She even went on to tell her Mother, "If you feel that you want to spend the rest of your life with David you should take the opportunity, should it arise."

Mary's relief was short-lived. When she later spoke to William she was rather taken aback by his rather hostile response. She was then unable to decide whether this was because William thought David would be trying to take his father's place, or whether he felt it was a threat to his position as man of the house. Whatever the reason, it was obvious to her that if ever the situation was to arise, she would have to keep the matter in abeyance for a while, if she was to maintain family harmony. For this reason she decided that there was no point in discussing the matter at all with her father-in-law.

Shortly afterwards, David screwed up his courage and proposed to her. Mary explained that although she was very touched by his proposal, and would have liked to be able to say, "Yes", she felt that it would not be fair to him, as the happy memories of her life with Bill would always come between them. She greatly valued their friendship, and hoped that they would continue to be great friends. David was, of course, very dejected at her answer but realised that he too would like to remain a firm family friend.

The next problem that was to cause Mary much soul searching occurred when Mary-Ann sat, and passed, her scholarship examination (later known as the 11+) and was offered a place at the High School in Taunton. Although Mary was receiving good wages for a woman, (although they were much less than David received for doing the same work) there was little money to spare after she had paid the rent, food for her growing family and all their clothing needs, plus her fares to work. For this reason she felt could not possibly manage to pay the school fees, and for Mary-Ann's school uniform.

At first she decided to tell Mary-Ann that, proud of her though she was, there was no way that she could find the money to send her to the High School. She then thought of the big sacrifices her in-laws had made to get her and Bill started in the bakery, and so she put off making any decision for a few days, which was just as well.

The following Sunday, after they had finished their meal, the washing up had been done, and both the children had gone out, Mary started to discuss the problem with her father-in-law. Much to her surprise he told her not to worry, but to leave the matter with him, as he thought he might be able to help her. With his wages and railway pension of only a few shillings a week, she had no idea how he would be able to do so, but she agreed to his request.

Two days later she received a letter through the post from Jon to tell her of a conversation with one of the many acquaintances that he talked to at the crossing gates. The man had informed him that many years ago a local benefactor had set up a trust fund to help children in the village who were in a similar position to Mary-Ann. He suggested she contacted the Clerk to the Parish Council, which she did. She was delighted when she was informed some four weeks later that the Trust fund would meet the costs incurred in providing Mary-Ann with the school uniform she needed, and that they would also help Mary with the school fees.

In the meantime, William realised that if his sister was at another school, her academic progress would no longer be compared to his own rather pedestrian efforts. To add financial weight to ensuring that this happened, he acquired two positions as an errand boy, working for one of the grocers in the village on Friday evenings, and for one of the butchers, on Saturday mornings.

He very quickly mastered the art of riding the rather cumbersome trade bicycles with their wicker basket that fitted into the tray over the smaller front wheel. Everyone who lived at the top end of the village knew when William had finished his round when he came down the hill at the end of the village, and along the High Street, past the football ground at a breakneck speed, with both feet off the pedals, before managing to pull up outside the grocer's, or the butcher's shop with much squealing of brakes. Each Friday and Saturday evening he solemnly handed over his wages to his Mother, keeping his tips (which often exceeded the wages he had been paid) for himself.

In September, Mary, her daughter and David, started to catch the 8.28am train from Bishops Lydeard into Taunton each weekday. Mary-Ann, unless she had extra lessons or hockey or netball matches, would catch the 4.40pm train back in the evening, and Mary would often find that her daughter had prepared a meal for the family and was getting on with her homework by the time she arrived home.

One Monday morning in October, Mary arrived at the office just before nine o'clock and found that Mr Leader had not yet arrived, which was most unusual because he was normally sitting at his desk, checking his watch to ensure that she was at her desk, and had started work on time. She thought nothing of it until about twelve o'clock when he had still not arrived, and she began to wonder if he had decided to take a holiday and not informed her.

When David collected her to go for their now customary dinner (lunch) break she asked him if he knew what had happened to Mr Leader, and was astonished to learn that neither Mr Forbes nor David had heard from him. By Wednesday of that week Mr Leader had still not put in an appearance in the office, nor had anyone heard of the reason for his absence. Surprised at the speed that she was able to clear her own work during his absence, Mary briefly thought about attempting to clear up some of the paperwork that was starting to accumulate on Mr Leader's desk. She quickly decided that she could not face the criticism she would receive on his return.

When he passed through her office later that afternoon Mr Forbes also noticed the growing pile of paperwork on Mr Leader's desk.

"Mary, do you think you could try to clear some of that arrears of paperwork?"

Mary hesitated before replying, "I did think I could, but what would Mr Leader say when he returns?"

"Don't worry about that: see what you can do, while I try to find out the reason for Mr Leader's absence."

"If you could spare David at any time to help me, I'd appreciate that," Mary added.

Mr Forbes nodded and smiled to himself as he returned to his own office, replying to her over his shoulder, "I'll see what can be arranged."

The following day Mary learned that Mr Forbes had called round to Mr Leader's house, and although he had not been able to see his employee, his wife had informed him that her husband had been unwell, but would definitely be returning to work the following Monday. With David's occasional help, Mary had managed to clear the entire back log of work by the time she went home the following Friday evening, thus ensuring that Mr Leader would return to a clear desk.

Because she was worrying about Mr Leader's reaction when he returned on Monday morning and realised that she had done his work, she found that she was unable sleep that night. She had also spent the entire weekend scolding the children, and ended her meeting with David on Saturday because of a trivial argument. She had to summon up all her courage to force herself to go into the office on the following Monday morning. When she arrived outside the office door it took her several minutes to screw up the courage to open it, only to find when she did so, that the cause of all her worries had still not put in an appearance.

She carried on coping with both her own and Mr Leader's work, with David's assistance, while the numerous letters sent by Mr Forbes to Mr Leader's home, remained unanswered. Mr Forbes then called at Mr Leader's house on several occasions, on his way home from work, but failed to get any reply when he rang the doorbell, and used the door knocker. Eventually deciding that the situation could not continue any longer, he went round to Mr Leader's house one afternoon, and continued to ring the doorbell, and use the door knocker until Mrs Leader eventually answered the door. In response to his request to see her husband Mrs Leader finally admitted that he was in hospital, and had been since the last day he had been at work.

After finding out the name of the ward he was in at the local hospital, and that the visiting hours were from 6.30pm to 7.00pm, Mr Forbes decided that he would visit Mr Leader in hospital, to find out what the real situation was. The following night when he arrived at the hospital, Mrs Leader was at her husband's bedside. Each patient was allowed only one visitor at a time, and Mrs Leader had already informed the Sister on the Ward that she would be staying at her husband's bedside until 7.00pm. Consequently, the nurse said that she was sorry but Mr Forbes would not be able to see his colleague that evening

He did, however, manage to speak to the Sister in charge of the ward. After he had explained why he needed to see her patient, the Sister informed him that Mr Leader had suffered a stroke, and he had lost the use of his right arm and leg, and was no longer able to speak clearly. Therefore it would be some time before he would be able to return to work, if at all.

By the following morning, when Mr Forbes arrived in the office, he had decided that, even if Mr Leader did return to work he would not be able to undertake the work he had been doing in the past. Therefore, alternative arrangements needed to be made to ensure the smooth running of the office. After informing David that from the following Monday morning he would be in charge of the Sales and Bought ledger department, he then called Mary in to his office.

"Mary, it has become evident that Mr Leader will not be returning to this office, or at least not in his previous capacity. I've already spoken to David, and put him in charge of the Sales and Bought ledger department. Likewise, from next Monday, I'd like you to work with me here in the Cashier's Office. However, until I find someone to replace you in the outer office, you will need to help David whenever possible, if you would."

Pleased at her unexpected promotion, Mary hardly knew how to thank Mr Forbes, before returning to her desk.

During the second week that she was working in the Cashier's office, Mary was helping David in his new office one afternoon. As they were clearing their desks before leaving to go home, she started to discuss with David a thought that had been going through her mind for the past few days.

"Why," she asked, "has the Company never considered treating both offices as one department? Then instead of trying to find a replacement clerk, why couldn't they take on a comptometer* operator and a typist instead, for far less money than a replacement for Mr Leader would cost in wages each week?"

She had not heard the door from the reception open. It was only when David gave her a warning glance as he looked towards the door, that she turned her head and saw that Mr Forbes had returned from his meeting with the Directors, and he had heard her comments. Blushing furiously, she darted into her office, collected her coat, and rushed out of the building as fast as she could go. When David managed to catch up with her, she was at least two hundred yards down the road and heading quickly towards the Station. Later, as she sat in the train compartment on the journey home, she could not hold back her tears; despite David's re-assurances, she did not believe that Mr Forbes had not heard her remarks.

In the morning when she arrived in the office it was only too obvious that Mr Forbes had heard what had been said, and before closing the door to the second office, he informed David that he did not wish to be disturbed until further notice. As soon as Mary had taken off her coat, he drew up a chair for her in front of his desk and indicated that she should sit down.

In an attempt to put her at ease he said, "I was very interested in your remarks last night, but unfortunately you dashed out of the office before I could discuss them with you: would you please outline your ideas in more detail."

By now Mary's mind was in a whirl; only a few months before she had been barely tolerated in the office, and, in her rather limited experience, only managers, who were always men, made decisions like that. He would probably regard any suggestions that she made as criticism, and would dismiss her. Realising that if she was dismissed there were not many firms would employ married women in their offices she wondered what she should do. Finally she convinced herself that she would not be in this mess if she had kept her mouth shut.

Her thoughts were interrupted when she heard Mr Forbes say, "Well?"

Blushing furiously, and still convinced that she was about to be dismissed, she decided to postpone the inevitable for as long as possible. She heard herself saying, "I'm sorry ... er ... I did not mean to ... er ... I should not have said ... er ... I don't know what you must think ..."

Realising that he was not going to get any sense from her while she was in her present distraught state, he told Mary to relax while he left the office for a few minutes. Pausing in the next office for a moment, he asked David what had upset Mary so much.

"She is convinced that she is about to be dismissed, if you heard what she said yesterday," David explained.

Mr Forbes was so astonished that he could only ask, "Why?"

David then had to explain. "She knows it isn't her place to express opinions on staffing matters – it was only an informal comment she made to me," he added, helpfully.

After a few minutes thought, Mr Forbes began to understand why someone in Mary's position would think that way, and realised that he would have to rethink his whole approach to the problem. Meanwhile, he asked David, "Could you possibly find a cup of tea from somewhere, and take it in to Mary. And then try to reassure her that she is not in any trouble. When you have succeeded in that," Mr Forbes concluded, "Would you please return and let me know?"

Thirty minutes later David returned, to inform Mr Forbes that Mary was feeling much better now. In the meantime, Mr Forbes had decided what his strategy would be.

When he entered the room and had sat down, his first words to Mary were, "Are you feeling better now?"

When she nodded in the affirmative he continued. "I have been thinking for some time that the working arrangements in these offices could be improved to the benefit of everyone. In the past I have discussed a number of proposals with Mr Leader who has always rejected my suggestions out of hand. I realised that without his agreement and co-operation it would be impossible to carry out any improvements." He hesitated then continued, "I feel we now have the opportunity to make a clean start and I want to hear what you have to say."

Thus re-assured, Mary explained what she had in mind. She said, "Both offices have busy times, and each office has to employ sufficient staff to cover their needs. In the Cashier's department the busy time is at the start of the month, when all the supplier's accounts have to be paid, whilst in the Sales and Bought Ledger departments, their busy period is in the last week of the month, when they have to clear all the remittance advice notes, and invoices to enable the Cashier's office to pay them at the start of the following month. Therefore, if the two offices were combined, it would result in a more consistent workload."

As he nodded his encouragement she continued, "By avoiding the need to employ another clerk, if the Company were to purchase a comptometer and employ an operator to use it, the comptometer operator would be able to check all the extensions on the invoices, etc., much more quickly than the present staff could do manually. It is also possible that she could undertake some work for other departments, for example the Wages department. If that proved feasible it would not be unreasonable to expect the wages department to contribute towards the comptometer operator's costs, thus reducing the wages bill of the accounts department still further."

Gaining in confidence, she finally suggested, "The Company should also obtain a typewriter and employ a typist who could type all the invoices, statements, advice notes etc., providing instant copies. That would avoid the need for all the documents to be hand-written and copies made as they are at the present moment." She then added, "The typist could also type out many of the numerous hand-written letters that are being sent out."

When she had finished, Mr Forbes sat there for a few minutes deep in thought, and then said, "What is the point of getting the typist to type the letter, if I have to write it out in longhand beforehand to enable her to type it?"

Mary promptly replied, "If you buy one of the new dictaphone* machines and train the typist to use it, you can dictate the letters into the machine even when the typist is not in the office, and she can then type them later."

After a further long pause Mr Forbes said, "How do you know so much about these modern devices?"

Mary replied that she had discussed the merits of the various items she had spoken about with the salesman, when she had seen them in the Office Equipment shop in the High Street, and he had demonstrated the equipment to her.

After what seemed like another long pause he rose to his feet.

"Thank you for all your help, Mary. May I ask you not to discuss your suggestions with anyone else in the Company for the time being." He then crossed the office to the door, and informed David that he was now free to receive visitors.

When they went out at mid-day for their meal, David questioned Mary closely about what had happened that morning, but apart from telling him that she had not been dismissed ... yet ... she told him she could not say anything else. Although her refusal to discuss the matter strained their relationship for a while, she was not prepared to break the undertaking that she had given to Mr Forbes.

When Mary returned to the office that afternoon she found that her boss had not gone out for anything to eat, and instead he was busy making copious notes, and numerous calculations, on a large pad, which he placed in the drawer of his desk whenever any one entered the room. At other times during the afternoon whenever she looked across at him, when he was not making notes, he was staring into space, apparently deep in thought.

On her arrival in the office the following morning she was astonished to find that Mr Forbes was already there, and was even more surprised when he said, "Don't take off your coat, Mary, because I want you to pay a visit to the Office Equipment shop with me."

That was nothing compared with the shock on David's face when, as they both went through his office. "David," Mr Forbes said, "We will both be out for a while, but should be back in about an hour's time."

As soon as they were out of the building Mr Forbes informed her that he wanted her to arrange for the salesman in the shop to give a demonstration of the machines she had spoken about. He wanted to see for himself the possible benefits of using this equipment. As the salesman demonstrated the machines, Mr Forbes asked more and more questions, but when he was finally satisfied that he had got all the information he needed, he thanked the salesman for his help as he left the shop. He also thanked Mary for her assistance as they walked back to the office.

Two days later Mr Forbes showed Mary a draft copy of the report that he intended to submit to the Directors, in which he had incorporated all the suggestions she had made, together with details of the savings that could be made. She also noted that unlike many Managers who tended to claim all the credit for ideas submitted by their staff, he had acknowledged the help she had given him.

Nothing more was heard of the suggestions that Mary had made for some months. Then one day David was called into the office and was told, with Mary, of the changes that were about to be made in the office procedures.

"Mary," Mr Forbes informed her, "You will be returning to your old office, but at Mr Leader's desk; David, you will return to the inner office at your old desk. The comptometer operator, together with her new machine, will be situated at Mary's old desk, and a new typist's desk, typewriter and Dictaphone machine has been purchased and will be installed in that office."

Then Mr Forbes informed Mary that the two new members of staff had been appointed. "They will be reporting to you next Monday morning and you will be responsible for the planning, and issuing of work to them. You will, of course, be getting an increase in your wages to cover your additional responsibilities." From the look of incredulity on David's face it was clear to Mr Forbes that Mary had followed his instructions not to discuss the proposals with anyone, and he made a mental note that he could rely on her in the future.

After some initial problems that were quickly sorted out by Mary, the work in the office soon settled into a routine and Mr Forbes found that all the benefits Mary had claimed were achieved. Costs were reduced; a greater volume of work was done in less time, and a more efficiently run office had been created without upsetting any members of the staff.

NEW EMPLOYMENT

The next year, 1923, was the year that William had been looking forward to, when at last he could leave school and start working full time. Having listened to his grandpa's tales the railways all of his life, he had thought, and every one else assumed, that he would get a job on the railway. Mr Morris, who seemed to have mellowed since Grandpa Jon had left the station, was only too happy to endorse William's application, adding that he was a hardworking and honest lad who would be a great benefit to the Company. He then forwarded both letters to the District Superintendent's office at Taunton.

A few days later William's dreams were shattered, when he received a reply informing him that there were no vacancies on the railway at this time. Although they would put his name on the list of applicants, they felt it only fair to inform him that priority would be given to young men whose fathers, or brothers, were already working for the Company. When he received a copy of the letter Mr Morris tried to find William, and when he failed to do so, he travelled up the line to Jon's cottage to inform him what had happened. After saying how sorry he was at the outcome, Mr Morris asked Jon to tell William when he saw him, that he would continue to try to find a job for him.

In the meantime William was contacting all the possible sources of employment in the village, but out of loyalty to his Mother the one firm that he did not contact was Smiths the bakers. He had learned that because of the new owner's dislike of hard work, and the inability of the new manager to get up in the morning, the firm had lost many of its most experienced staff. They had simply got fed up waiting outside the bake-house every morning throughout the year for the premises to be opened, before they could start work. For this reason, the quality of the bread was, to put it mildly, rather variable. Either because of a lack of time due a late start, or to the absence of members of staff, there were often insufficient supplies of bread to meet the needs of one shop, let alone two. This meant that the virtual monopoly of bread supplies in the village the firm had enjoyed when his father was manager, ceased when others saw an opportunity to supply bread to those customers who were dissatisfied with the service they were getting from Smiths.

Unfortunately, neither of the other two Bakers, nor the Wheelwright, the Plumber, the two Butchers, the Saddler and Harness maker, the Basket Maker, the two motor mechanics, or any of the numerous Carpenters, or Blacksmiths in the Village could offer him any employment at that time. One day William was wandering disconsolately along Taunton Road, kicking every loose stone that he saw. As he passed the entrance to the engineering premises he noticed out of the corner of his eye a note pinned to the gatepost at the entrance to the works. At first he ignored it, but then his curiosity overcame him and he turned back to read the notice which said:

LAD WANTED FOR YARD WORK – APPLY WITHIN

Tearing the note off the post so that no one else would have the chance to apply for the job before him, he raced through the gate and he was soon knocking on the door of the bungalow that stood in the corner of the yard and was used as an office.

The owner of the Company, who was known to everyone in the village as AK, was in the office when William arrived out of breath at the door. Because AK had lived in the village all his life, he had known William's father, and also remembered his mother from the time when she had served him in the baker's shop, so he was anxious to help the family by offering William a job if he could. After explaining to William what he would be required to do, and satisfying himself that William would be able to cope with the work, AK. offered him the job, and asked him if he could start the following morning. After confirming that he would be able to do so, William ran all the way home to tell the family of his good fortune and was disappointed when he got home to find that neither his sister nor his mother had returned home and that it would be at least two hours before he could tell the family of his good news.

AK was the owner of a farm on the edge of the village, and some years earlier had been the first farmer in the area to acquire a new traction engine and threshing machine, to enable him to harvest his crops. Finding that he had gathered in his own harvest, whilst his neighbours were still attempting to clear theirs, he decided that because his equipment was standing idle, he would hire out the new plant to his neighbours, to enable them to finish their harvesting before the weather broke.

From this small beginning the contracting side of his business had, over the years, acquired more threshing machines, traction engines, steam rollers, steam lorries, and a quarry from which stone was extracted for road making. To house all this additional equipment many of the original farm buildings had been converted into workshops, garages, store rooms, and a smithy's shop.

At first young William's task was to keep the yard swept and tidy, clearing the ash and char, that had been deposited on the ground when the fires were dropped from the traction engines, rollers, and lorries. William was soon to find out that he was expected to shovel this waste material into sacks, so that it could then be used as hard-core for pavements and paths etc. Another one of his many tasks was to stack the coal when it was unloaded in the yard, and he soon learnt how to build a wall with the larger lumps of coal to ensure that the remainder of the coal was retained in a well defined area.

He also found he was expected to empty the fireboxes of ash and clinker and the char from the smoke-boxes, clear the boiler tubes on all the vehicles, clean the bodywork including the wheels, and even underneath the mudguards if they were fitted, polish all the brasswork on the engines and lorries until they sparkled. While William was engrossed in his work AK would sometimes be seen standing outside the office door watching his progress. Often when William had finished AK would stroll over to the vehicle that William had been working on, and closely check the work that he had just completed. If AK was satisfied with the standard of William's work he would say, "Well done son," but if he saw any blemishes on either the paintwork, or the brasswork, he would quickly point them out to William, and then he would wait around until the work was completed to his satisfaction.

Soon William was also checking that all the vehicles in the yard had enough water in their tanks, and their boilers, that the fires were lit in the fireboxes, and that the boiler pressure was adequate to ensure that the safety valves were just simmering whenever a vehicle was due to leave the yard. William was never quite sure how he had finished up with the last job, but at least it meant that he had less time to act as 'gofor' for the fitter, or the blacksmith, or act as tea boy whenever anyone needed a cuppa.

One sunny morning in Summer when the yard was empty, because every available machine was in use, the fitter employed by the company drove into the yard in AK's Humber car bringing it to a sudden halt in a cloud of dust, close to the spot where William was sacking up a pile of ash. Telling him to jump into the car, as soon as William had closed the car door, the fitter put the car into gear and drove out of the yard at a furious pace. As they went down the road Alf the fitter explained that one of the local farmers had been on the telephone to AK complaining that one of the firm's threshing machines had broken down, and the farmer was threatening to terminate his leasing contract.

When they arrived at the farm at Cothelstone, William found out why his presence had been needed. Alf quickly discovered that the farmer, in his haste to get the harvest cleared in the shortest possible time, so he could reduce AK's hire charges to a minimum, had instructed his farm hands to pile as much hay as they possibly could through the thresher and bailer at any one time. From many years of experience his farm hands knew that if they carried out his instructions to the letter there would soon be a breakdown, but they also knew that, with the mood the farmer was in that morning it was no use arguing with him, so they set to with a will, and when the inevitable happened, they were able to sit down and enjoy a well-earned drop of cider while they waited for the fitter to arrive.

As soon as Alf and William arrived and they saw what had happened, Alf disconnected all the drive belts to ensure that nothing on the threshing machine or the baler could move. He then told William to crawl through a narrow gap into the confined space inside the machine and push out the straw, stones and other debris that had caused it to jam, while Alf prised open the rollers at the other side to clear the blockage. Once all the debris was cleared out, and William had emerged from the confined space inside the machine some 45 minutes later, the belts were slipped back on and the thresher was restarted.

This particular day was the hottest day of the year, and after William had emerged from the machine, he was sweating profusely, his shirt was wringing wet, and he was grateful to one of the farmhands for the offer of a drop of cider to quench his thirst. He was able to stand around for a while as his shirt dried out in the heat from the sun, while Alf persuaded the farmer that he should not encourage his labourers to cause another blockage of the equipment, because he would have to pay for any damage caused to the machines by his negligence. As soon as the farmer was satisfied that the equipment was again operating properly, Alf and William climbed back into the car to return to the works. Afterwards William was often called to help the fitter, both in the workshop and on emergency calls. The blacksmith also began to appreciate William's help.

END OF AN ERA

The following year, 1924, Mary returned from work one Friday evening to see a policeman standing on her doorstep. Unaware that Mary-Ann had already arrived home, and was in fact upstairs doing her homework, Mary immediately assumed that her daughter had been involved in an accident. When the policeman told her, "Sorry, Madam, I have some bad news for you – could I please step inside?" she began to fear the worst.

After the policeman had closed the door he told her, "It's your father-in-law, Ma'am. He was found dead at his crossing keeper's cottage this morning."

Relief that her daughter was safe, soon turned to sadness when she realised that Jon was not only her father-in-law, but a real friend, who had helped her through so many of the crises in her life, from the time when she and Bill had wanted to marry and he encouraged them to take over the management of the bakery shop; when Bill was killed; when she had been dismissed from the bakery, and to when Mary-Ann had passed her exams.

As soon as she had shown the policeman out of the door Mary burst in to tears, sobbing uncontrollably in the kitchen, as she realised that she would no longer be able to turn to Jon for advice. The first indication that Mary-Ann had that anything was wrong, was when she heard her mother crying downstairs, and she rushed down to find out what was wrong. It took some time for Mary-Ann to find out from her distraught mother what had happened, and when she did so, she also started to cry.

William was late home that evening because of yet another emergency at the works, and when he arrived he found the stationmaster Mr Morris, talking to his mother and sister. He noticed that both his mother and sister had tear-stained cheeks, and red eyes from crying. He then learned of the death of his grandpa, and that the stationmaster had called to offer them all his condolences.

"I've made arrangements," Mr Morris said, "for Jon's body to be taken to the local Chapel of Rest. I'm sorry to have to tell you this, but the railway company wants all of Jon's belongings out of the cottage by tomorrow: it's so that a replacement keeper can move in, you see. We have to have a man there."

In an attempt to help Mary, Mr Morris had offered to send round the railway carrier's cart the following morning with a driver, to collect Mary and the children, and then take them all up to the cottage. He would then help them to pack the contents, and bring them back to Mary's house and unload it. Mr Morris also offered to store any furniture at the station, that Mary could not find room for in her own house, until she could make other arrangements. After Mary had thanked Mr Morris for his kind offer, he departed, confirming that he would see her in the morning.

William then sat down in a chair in the corner of the kitchen deep in his thoughts, remembering the many happy times he had spent in the past with his grandpa, the days in the signal box, the trips on the footplate, his grandpa's tales of life on the railway. As he remembered those moments, he too was overcome with grief but, still unable to show his emotions in front of the women, he had to rush upstairs so his mother and sister would not see him crying.

No-one in the family felt like eating that night, and after what was to be a sleepless night for all of them, the carrier's van arrived early the following morning with Mr Morris, out of his usual uniform, driving the cart. Once they arrived at their destination, he insisted on helping with the packing, and loading, of the van. As the day wore on it became very hot, and Mary decided that they all deserved a cup of tea. After she had made it she was sitting on a packing case sipping her tea in the front room, while all the others sat drinking theirs in the sun in the small front garden. Looking around the little room, she noticed a beautiful china teapot standing on the mantelpiece, that she had seen, and liked, from the moment Bill had first taken her to his home, to meet his parents, all those years ago.

Putting down her cup she walked over to the mantelpiece to examine the teapot more closely, as she held it in her hands she thought that when she got it home, it would take pride of place in her small china cabinet as a lasting memory of Jon. Her joy at the discovery was almost short lived, because she nearly dropped the teapot when she opened the lid and discovered five crisp new white £5 notes inside together with a hand-written note in the copper plate handwriting that she knew so well.

The card said simply, "Mary this money should cover my funeral expenses." Once again she was overcome with emotion, and had to put the teapot she treasured so much back on the mantelpiece again, before she dropped it, as she struggled to regain her composure. It was a long time before she was calm enough to pick up that teapot again without fear of dropping it.

After the house had been emptied and the keys handed over to Mr Morris, Mary held on to that teapot all the way home, not because of the money that it still contained, but simply to ensure that no harm would come to it. The return journey seemed to take a very long time, during which no one spoke, because each person was immersed in their own thoughts of the man they had all regarded as a friend, a grandfather, and a mentor.

The following day, a Sunday, Mary went down to David's house when she knew that he would be at home, and told him what had happened. She then asked him to explain to Mr Forbes that she would be a little late into the office the following morning, because she had to make all the funeral arrangements, but that she would be in as soon as possible, and would stay late to make up for any time that she had lost.

As soon as William learned that the funeral had been arranged for the following Thursday he approached AK for time off from work to attend his grandpa's funeral, and was upset to see a smile briefly cross his employer's face. Realising that he had upset the boy AK quickly explained.

"I've heard that excuse so many times before by young lads trying to get time off from work, but on this occasion I know your request is genuine. In fact," he added, "I shall also be attending the service, for I knew you grandpa for many years."

Concerned that her absence from school would jeopardise her daughter's chances in the forthcoming examinations, Mary suggested to her that perhaps it would be best if she went to school, rather than attending the funeral. Mary-Ann would not hear of it, and after she had handed in a note to her teacher explaining the reason her absence, she took her place at the service beside her mother and her brother.

As Mary sat with her children in the congregation listening to the solitary bell tolling, while she waited for the bearers to enter the Church with the coffin, she glanced at the rectangular war shrine in the chancel and wondered how her Bill would have coped in the situation she now found herself in. She was surprised to see that by the time the service was due to start, the Church was full with many people that she knew from the Village, and the railway. She also noted that Jon was the last surviving member of his generation of the Hawkes, and Pearce families in the district. After the service was over, the Rev Fitch led the congregation to the graveside where his body was laid to rest.

Another tradition that Mary found that she could no longer maintain when the service had finished were the sumptuous refreshments that had been available at all the funerals organised by her side of the family in the past. This tradition had ceased when rationing was introduced during the Great War and did not appear to have been revived. Mary had, however, arranged for a small reception to be held for Jon's closest friends in the Village Hall, and after making certain that everything was satisfactory, she made her apologies before leaving with her daughter for the station to catch the 11.56am train to take them back to work, and school.

PROMOTIONS

Three years later, in 1927, the Hawkes family encountered their next major problem when Mary-Ann sat, and passed her scholarship examination, thus enabling her to continue her education in the sixth form at the High School. Mary-Ann was worried at first whether her mother could afford to let her continue with her studies, or whether she should start to look for work. But she was reassured when her mother informed her that she had been promised they would continue to receive a grant towards the cost of her uniform so that she could continue with her studies.

As for Mary's job, the volume of work at the shirt factory continued to increase, and more machinists were taken on, which resulted in a corresponding increase in the amount of work that the offices had to undertake. Shortly after the re-organisation had been completed, the company found that, as Mary had predicted, all the wages calculations could also be carried out on the new comptometer machines which had been introduced.

During the next few months the number of ledger entries, invoices, advice notes, and statements, continued to increase. This meant more clerical staff needed to be employed as bookkeepers. At first the extra staff were accommodated in the existing buildings, but as their numbers continued to grow it soon became apparent that the existing office space would be insufficient.

Rumours began to circulate that the company was planning to open another factory in the town. These stories seemed to gain credence when it was learned that Mr Forbes, who had been about to retire, had been asked by the Directors to remain with the Company for a further two years. Mary was also concerned that with two comptometer operators, two typists, and another bought ledger clerk (also female) to supervise, she was struggling to cope with what she regarded as her own work as well. The rather cramped conditions in her office did not help either, and it was no consolation to her when she learned that the conditions in the other offices were hardly any better.

During this same period, the company that William worked for also continued to expand, and additional lorries, rollers, and threshers, together with the most recent addition to the fleet of a petrol-driven tractor, had all been acquired since William had started. The number of extra vehicles meant that William was no longer able to keep the whole of the yard tidy on his own, and AK had taken on another lad to help him. William was still responsible for dropping the fires in the engines and lorries, cleaning the fire and smoke-boxes and the boiler tubes. His assistant helped him clean the paintwork and polish the brasses. William was also allowed to drive the vehicles from the workshops into the garage area, after the fitters had finished working on them. He was soon spending a lot of his time helping the fitter in the workshops, or working with him on outside jobs. Later he found that he was coming in to work long before the others were due to start, simply to ensure that the vehicles were in steam and ready to depart at 8am.

During the time that William had been employed by the company he had received regular wage increases, an indication not only of his increasing value to the Company, but also how much his efforts were appreciated. He now found that, not only was he providing his mother with sufficient money for the rent and his keep, but he could also afford to buy himself some smart clothes, and go for the occasional night out with his friends at the Bell Hotel, or the Lethbridge Arms, if he was not working.

During the next year, 1928, it was finally announced to the employees at Mary's company that the shirt factory would be opening other premises nearby. There they would manufacture a new type of shirt with a semi stiff collar, which had been invented in America, instead of the type of shirts they had been producing. The office staff were also informed by the management that all the offices would remain on the present site, until the new administration block was built, when all the offices would be moved into the new building, with the accounts department occupying one large office on the first floor.

After the new office block was completed, and the changeover had been accomplished, Mr Forbes announced that he was about to retire, and all the staff were informed that David had been appointed Manager of the enlarged accounts department in his place. That evening when Mary was walking to the station with David she congratulated him on his promotion.

"Don't you worry," he replied, "you'll be all right."

She was surprised by this and wondered whatever he could mean.

She was soon to learn exactly what he meant when Mr Forbes called her into his office a few days later.

"Let me explain what is going to happen," he said to her. "We have decided to expand both the typist and comptometer sections to cope with the increased workload. You, Mary, will be responsible for interviewing and engaging the extra staff required, together with a replacement supervisor, who will take over the job you have been doing."

Hearing of this decision, Mary could only look at Mr Forbes in open-mouthed surprise, wondering what on earth he was going to say next. She received an even bigger shock when he continued, "The Directors wish to appoint a Company Personnel Officer, and they have decided that you should be offered the post."

Mary was so astounded that all she could whisper was, "Why me?"

Mr Forbes smiled.

"In your new position you will have all the personal details of every member of the staff working for the company, and because of the need to ensure that this information remained secure, it is essential that the company appoint a person that they could trust. That person is you, Mary. I have not forgotten the time when the first office reorganisation took place: I had asked you not to mention any details of the planned office reorganisation to anyone. When I announced the changes I realised from the expression on David's face that although he was a friend of yours, you had not mentioned a single word to him."

Mary blushed a little.

Mr Forbes then continued, "When I learnt of the Director's proposals to recruit someone from outside the company for the post of Company Personnel Officer, I suggested to the Directors that you should be offered the post, and after I had outlined the reasons for my proposal, I was pleased to learn later that they had accepted my recommendations."

In her new position Mary was to receive a substantial salary increase (she was now to be paid a monthly salary instead of receiving a weekly wage); she was also to have her own separate office for security reasons. Her secretary would be situated in the outer office, and would be responsible for arranging all Mary's appointments. Another sign of the seniority of her new position was that she was to have one of the very few internal telephones that the company had recently acquired, together with another telephone with a direct outside line to the local telephone exchange. It was now David's turn to congratulate Mary, and to surprise her when she learned that he too could keep a secret. He had known of her imminent promotion for some time.

When demands were received from the various managers in the company for new or replacement members of staff, it was Mary's task to recruit people with the right skills, and to arrange for them to be trained, if they did not have suitable qualifications. Before long many of the managers began to appreciate her ability to recruit the type of person they were looking for, without the need for them to interview numerous unsuitable candidates.

There was, however, one exception. She often thought she had obtained a ideal candidate for one particular manager, only to learn that she was required to start searching all over again, because for various reasons, this individual did not consider the person that Mary had sent down to him to be suitable.

At first Mary could not understand why so many of these candidates, all of whom had suitable qualifications, were not acceptable. Then one day, in desperation, she sent an applicant who had been rejected by Mr James (the Manager who was causing Mary so many problems), to another department which had a similar vacancy. Mary was pleasantly surprised to learn thirty minutes later from Mr Groves, the manager of the section, that the applicant, who had been rejected by Mr James, was ideal and was the sort of person Mr Groves had been seeking for some time.

Anxious to get to the bottom of the matter Mary asked her secretary to ring Mr James, and inform him that she wished to discuss this problem with him in her office.

Three days later Mary was reminded by Pearl, her secretary, that although she had contacted Mr James on a number of occasions to remind him that Mary still wanted to see him, she had not received any positive response from him. Mary decided that she had wasted enough time, and after checking with Pearl that she had no appointments for the next thirty minutes, she went straight downstairs to see Mr James. After observing through the open door of his office that he was not engaged, and appeared to be simply gazing into space while he smoked a cigarette, she went through the open door and closed it behind her.

After waiting in vain for him to offer her a seat, or to rise to his feet as she entered the office, as Mr Forbes would have done, she was absolutely furious. Determined not to let Mr James see how annoyed she was, she said in a quiet voice, "I take it that you must be extremely busy, Mr James," to which he nonchalantly replied, "Not especially."

This was the opening she had been looking for. Mary said, "But presumably you have been very busy for the past two days."

Not realising the trap that she was setting for him, he once again replied, "Not especially."

Until now Mr James had been slouching in his chair, but Mary's next remark made him sit up with a jerk. "Then will you please explain why you have failed to respond to my requests for you to come to my office, and discuss the problem we seem to have finding new recruits for your department."

Going red in the face, Mr James jumped out of his chair and shouting so loudly that many people outside the office heard him, said, "I am not running around after any bloody woman, nor am I going to take orders from a woman like you."

Mary realised there was no possibility of holding a reasoned, or rational discussion with him, and said as she turned to leave his office, "Very well Mr James, as I cannot determine the reasons why you consider so many of the applicants I send to you as unsuitable, I will refrain from sending you any more. I consider that you are being unreasonable and I cannot understand why you feel that you need to humiliate people in this way. I shall also be informing the Directors of the reasons for my decision."

Before she could close the door behind her, it was wrenched out of her grasp, by the now almost apoplectic Mr James, who knocked her against the wall as he pushed past her, and then ran up the stairs to the offices on the floor above.

After recovering her composure Mary returned to her office, and as she passed through Pearl's office asked her to come in with her shorthand notebook, when she had finished the letter she was typing. As Mary sat trying to compose her thoughts before Pearl's arrival, she became aware of the increasingly obtrusive sound of raised voices, coming from one of the offices along the corridor. When she paused to listen for a moment, she realised that it was Mr James who was doing all the shouting. At that moment Pearl entered to take the letter Mary wished to dictate, and already aware through the grapevine of what had happened downstairs, she said mischievously, "I think that is Mr James shouting, I wonder what has upset him?"

Mary quietly replied, "I wonder!" before starting to dictate her letter.

After she had dictated her letter, Mary sat wondering how she was going to resolve the immediate problem she was faced with, together with the many others she was expected to solve, when she heard the sound of her office door being quietly closed. Looking up she saw that it was the tall white-haired, well-groomed figure of Mr Lowdnes the new

Managing Director, who had only recently joined the Company. After firmly shutting the door behind him, he pulled up a chair, and then sat down facing her.

"Could you spare a few minutes to discuss a problem with me?" When she nodded in the affirmative he continued, "I believe you had an altercation earlier this afternoon, and I would like you to tell me what happened please."

After determining that he was referring to her recent meeting with Mr James, Mary explained precisely what had happened. When she finished, Mr Lowdnes sat deep in thought for a while, he then said to Mary, "Why did you ask him to come up to your office?"

Mary replied, "I did so, because I thought that there was less chance of our conversation being overheard by other parties." After another long pause Mr Lowdnes said, "So it was not, as Mr James has suggested, done simply to humiliate him." Mary was so shocked and annoyed at this suggestion, which had never crossed her mind, that all she could do was to shake her head to indicate her denial.

"Thank you for your help, Mary," said Mr Lowdnes, then rose and left her office, pausing for a moment to speak to Pearl before returning to his own office.

After his departure Mary turned her attention to drafting a 'situations vacant' notice for the local newspaper. Once again her thoughts were interrupted when Mr Lowdnes' secretary rang, and informed Mary that the MD wished to see her in his office immediately. After telling Pearl where she was going, Mary tried to gather her thoughts together as she walked the short distance down the corridor to his office. When Mary arrived, his secretary looked up.

"You are expected, please go straight in," she said.

As she entered, Mr Lowdnes rose to his feet, and as she was shutting the door he pulled up a chair for her, and when she had sat down, he returned to his own seat. After looking at her for what she thought was ages, but in reality was only a few seconds, he said, "Mrs Hawkes, I have to tell you that I was against your appointment to the position of Company Personnel Officer. Apart from the responsibilities involved, I felt certain that the possibility of the kind of situation that you experienced today was bound to occur, and that it was unreasonable to expect any woman to cope with this type of situation. The other Directors were persuaded by Mr Forbes that you were quite capable of dealing with any problems that might arise, and although I voted against your appointment I found myself in a minority of one and accepted their decision."

He continued, "I understand that, through no fault of yours, the scenario I feared would happen did take place this afternoon. Apart from the complainant, everyone else that I have spoken to was very impressed with the manner in which you handled the situation. You did not inform me that you had been sworn at, or that you were knocked to one side by Mr James, and I must apologise on behalf of the Company, that you were treated in this manner. The Board, and I, are not prepared to tolerate behaviour of this kind from any member of our staff." He then added, "In an attempt to ensure that neither you nor any other member of the staff will be treated in this manner in the future, I have given instructions that Mr James is to be dismissed immediately for gross misconduct, and he is now being escorted off the premises."

When Mary learned what had happened, she was upset that a married man with a family had been dismissed because of a course of action she had initiated, and found herself asking Mr Lowdnes if it was really necessary for him to go. It was only then that she learned that there had been a number of complaints in the past about his attitude, both from present, past, and potential new members of staff.

"Still, I am sorry that the incident has turned out this way," she said firmly.

"In future," Mr Lowdnes went on, "I will be arranging monthly meetings with you, in an attempt to avoid any recurrence of such an incident."

Later, when she was in a reflective mood, Mary realised that this incident was probably the turning point of her career with the company. It crossed her mind that in the past many members of the management team may have thought, when she was appointed to her post, that the job had been created simply to appease the trade unions, who were recruiting more members within the factory at the time. Others who did not know her, might have felt that this was another example of someone being promoted simply because they were incapable of doing the job they had been given, and moved into a post where it was thought they would do less harm, a common practice in many companies at the time. Other members of the staff may have thought that Mary had been appointed simply to look after the interests of the Directors, rather than theirs.

After the incident with Mr James had been resolved, she noticed a change in the attitude towards both her, and the job she was doing, not only by the directors and managers, but also by the members of staff. The Management team appeared to appreciate the benefits Mary was bringing to the company. For the first time the company had a waiting list of people who wanted to work in the factory, and the staff realised that she was prepared to look after their interests as well

Shortly afterwards, Mr Forbes, who had retired some months earlier, came into the factory on one of his regular visits. He liked to satisfy himself that the reorganisation he had initiated was still operating satisfactorily, and that his proteges, as he liked to call them (Mary and David), were carrying out their duties in the manner that he expected of them. When he was shown into Mary's office, he sat down and wasted no time before questioning her about the difficulties she had experienced with Mr James.

After she had outlined what had happened, he continued to question her, and finally he said, "And what did Mr Lowdnes say to you?" At first Mary tried to avoid answering the question, but after further probing from 'the old man', (as he was known throughout the works), she admitted that Mr Lowdnes had informed her that he had originally been opposed to her appointment, because he thought that the job was too stressful for a woman. On hearing this, he chuckled, then he leaned over the desk towards her and whispered, "Well he didn't know you like I did. Can I take it that he finally admitted that he made a mistake?" In response to this observation Mary merely nodded her head and smiled.

After he had finished his cup of tea, and had left her office to see David, Mary sat for a while thinking that although he had retired, he still retained his immaculate, but rather old-fashioned appearance, with his black jacket and waistcoat, pin striped trousers, his fresh white shirt with the stiff starched winged collar, and his impeccable old-world mannerisms. The only thing that was missing from the days when he worked at the factory was the furled umbrella he had carried in every day.

As she sat deep in thought after he left she found herself wondering how he managed to keep in daily touch with all that was happening in the works, even though he only visited the site about once every four weeks. She also realised once again that his appearance belied his razor sharp mind, his knowledge of how people reacted, and the fact that in so many ways his thinking was ahead of his time. She recalled how, many years before, he had realised that the old autocratic style of management was doomed to failure, and that any company would only get the best from its workers by providing them with the most efficient equipment to enable them to carry out their work, and by treating their staff as partners, if they were to succeed in the modern world

Like many others in the company who had known him, she was stunned when four weeks later she learnt that Mr Forbes had died peacefully in his sleep. Well aware of the debt that she owed him, she was pleased when she was asked, together with David, to represent the company at his funeral. She thought that as she had attended a number of funerals recently, and that as he was not a close relative, she would be able to keep her emotions under control. Yet as she sat in the Church listening to the funeral oration, she broke down and cried bitterly when she realised that she had lost yet another dear friend and colleague, and that never again would he be there to help her.

RECESSION TIMES

Although it did not escape the effects of the recession, Somerset was not so badly affected by the slump of the 1930s as many other parts of the country. The towns around the Somerset coalfields were affected. In the village, it was the farming community that suffered, and this of course, had a knock-on effect on the rest of the community.

Many small farmers unable to obtain an economic price for either their crops, milk, or their livestock, simply decided that they could no longer carry on, and surrendered the leases on their farms on the next quarter day. Others did not survive until then. A number of the larger farmers like AK. managed to buy either the leases of the smaller farms, or the farms themselves, if they adjoined their lands. At the same time they often bought either the desperate farmer's standing crops, or his livestock, for knockdown prices. A lot of farm machinery lay rusting in the open or in barns, as it cost more to arrange the auction, than the unfortunate farmer was likely to get for the implements themselves. Some machinery did come on to the market, and AK acquired two, almost new, International tractors at bargain prices primarily for his own use, although he was always prepared to hire them out.

Because of the reduced demand for all equipment used in the farming industry AK decided that, if any of his older units required major repairs, or an expensive overhaul, it would be more economical to scrap them, after salvaging any parts that could be used as spares to maintain the rest of the fleet. He could then obtain more modern plant for less than the cost of the repairs. By now William was employed virtually full time as a fitter, and he often had the dismal job of condemning, and dismantling many of the machines he had lovingly looked after for many years.

One consolation was that AK's steam rollers were in constant use. The Government of the day, working with the County Council, set about the task of improving many of the roads in the County by using a number of workers who would otherwise be unemployed, and claiming the dole. Anyone who went to the local Labour Exchange to sign on was expected, provided they were physically fit, to work on these projects, even if they had no previous experience of heavy manual work. If they refused to undertake this work they could not obtain any unemployment benefit.

If there was not enough work for William in the yard, or if no-one else was available, he would be expected to drive the roller to the site of the roadworks, and work with the road repair gang levelling the base, and later the tarmac surface of the road. He soon became aware of just how desperate some of these men must have been to have undertaken this work. Unemployed coal miners were more used to hard manual work, and adapted more easily to the task, but many others had never undertaken such physical work in their lives before. Some had been previously employed as clerks, or shop assistants, and they struggled to cope with the work they were expected to do.

The passing of the Road Traffic Act in 1930 had resulted in a considerable increase in the amount of work undertaken by the haulage section of the business, which was the only section that was continuing to expand. To cope with the increased traffic that was on offer, AK decided to replace the steam lorries with new ERF motor lorries. As they arrived it soon became obvious that with no fire, tubes, or smoke boxes to clean, grates to clear, or coal and water to replace, the new vehicles would require far less maintenance than the steam lorries they were replacing, and William began to wonder how long it would be before he too, joined the lengthening dole queues.

One day a new lorry was delivered, and the driver who had brought the lorry down from the factory parked it in the entrance to the yard, and switched off the engine so preventing any other vehicles from entering or leaving. Climbing down from the cab he asked William, who happened to be standing nearby, the way to the railway station, then handed over the keys of the lorry to him, before running down to the station as fast as he could go to catch the next train home. Realising that the vehicle could not be left where it was, William climbed up into the cab, and as soon as he had familiarised himself with the controls he switched on the engine, put the lorry into gear, and then drove it further in to the yard, before reversing to park it next to the one remaining steam lorry.

What William had not realised, was that AK had come out of the office in the yard to inspect his new acquisition, just in time to see his young employee climb up into the cab. He then watched as William parked the lorry as if he had been driving these new vehicles all his life. When William had completed this task and switched off the engine, he sat in the cab for a moment, before climbing down, to return to his work. Suddenly the near side door opened and AK climbed up into the cab. Looking straight at William he said, "So you think that you can drive one of these new lorries, young man?" William, who thought he was in trouble, tried to think of a suitable reply, but before he could do so AK continued, "Let's see what you can do then; take me for a ride, but remember it's a new vehicle."

Nervously switching on the engine, he put the vehicle in gear, drove slowly to the yard entrance and after turning left onto the main road he drove towards Taunton, before turning right at the Cross Keys public house. He then went through Norton Fitzwarren Village, and along the Barnstaple road, before turning right again through Halse, even managing to negotiate the sharp right hand bend outside the New Inn. Then he went across Ash Common, before returning to the village over the bridge that crossed the railway line near the station. As he did so he invoked the fury of Mr Morris, the stationmaster who considered that these new lorries were far too heavy for his bridge, but as the bridge itself showed no sign of imminent collapse the incident was soon forgotten. William then continued on his way into the village, turning right in Gore Square and then left into the yard, finally parking the lorry back in the space he had driven it from earlier.

After applying the handbrake, putting the lorry into neutral gear, and switching off the engine there was a brief pause before AK said quietly, "Well done lad, I'll make you up to a driver as soon as I can." (There was no National driving test at this time). When all the new motor lorries had been delivered, a couple of the old fellows in their sixties who had driven the steam lorries for many years were given the opportunity to drive the new motor vehicles, but after attempting to do so, claimed that they "would never be able to get on with they darned modern things."

Both of the old fellows had worked for AK for many years, and he knew that if he dismissed them, they would be unlikely to find another job at their age, unless it was working on the road gangs, the prospect of which AK could not even contemplate. So he was faced with a problem. After a great deal of thought he decided to give Alf, who was William's long time assistant in the yard, a trial as a driver, and when he proved to be satisfactory, he made him up to a driver together with William. This enabled the two old men to work out the remaining time before their retirement, helping out in the yard. Soon afterwards both of the young lads, William and Alf, found themselves travelling around parts of the Somerset countryside they had never seen before.

A CHALLENGE

It was in 1930 that Mary-Ann sat and passed her Matriculation Examination, achieving honours in all subjects. Mary's excitement at her daughter's achievements soon turned to anger when she later asked her daughter what plans she had made for the future. Mary-Ann replied that she had hoped to go to University, and from there to Medical School to train as a doctor, but supposed she would have to settle for a career in nursing because it appeared that was all women were considered to be suitable for.

When Mary learnt that her daughter had applied to four Universities and been rejected by all of them without even being granted an interview, she found herself shouting at her daughter, "You must not give up trying; if you give in now other women who try to follow in your footsteps in the future, will find it even more difficult to be accepted."

After calming down Mary realised from the look on her daughter's face that she had not convinced her of the need to continue to try for a place at University. Mary was still pondering on the problem as she left the Station with David on her way home from work two days later. Coming out of the station building, as she turned right to climb up the steps to the road that led into the village, Mary was vaguely aware of someone sitting in a trap outside the station. She was surprised when the person in the trap said, in a voice that she recognised from many years ago, "Mary may I have a word with you, please?"

She stopped, and, seeing who it was, said to David, "Do go on, don't wait for me." Then she turned back to speak to Mrs Smith, the widow of her former boss Bert the baker. As Mary arrived alongside the trap Mrs Smith said, "Don't stand there, do come up here please, dear, I can't possibly say what I need to, if you remain down there."

As Mary climbed up into the trap she wondered what on earth could be so important that Mrs Smith could not have put in a letter, and why she had decided that it was necessary to drive all the way to the station to meet her, instead of meeting her at home. She did not have much time to ponder on these thoughts because as soon as she sat down in the trap, she was asked, "What is this I hear about your daughter not wanting to go to University when she has the opportunity to do so?"

Wondering how on earth Mrs Brown had obtained this information, at the same time trying hard not to lose her temper, Mary snapped back at Mrs Smith, "It is not that she does not want to go to university, it is simply that she is not being given the opportunity to do so because she is a woman."

Mrs Smith calmly asked, "How many Universities has she applied to?"

Mary snapped back, "Four, but how many does she need to apply to and not get an answer from before she realises that there is no way she is ever going to be allowed to achieve her aims?"

Mrs Smith replied, "I am disappointed in you Mary, I never thought that you would give in so easily. From what I hear you have done well in a man's world, and I am surprised that you have allowed your daughter to give up without a fight. Does she usually give in easily?"

Stung by this rebuke Mary was so furious she was about to descend from the trap, but before she could do so, the pony was coaxed into a fast trot because Mrs Smith decided at that moment she could not let the matter rest. As the horse trotted quickly down the station drive Mrs Smith said, "I think that I had better have a word with that young lady of yours, and there is no time like the present; is she at home now?"

On being told that she was, the pony was coaxed into an even faster trot, slowing down only slightly, to negotiate the sharp bend out of the station drive on to the main road into the village.

Clinging on to the side rail of the trap in an attempt to ensure that she was not thrown out of the trap as they went round each bend in the road, they passed David, long before he had reached Gore Square. As they went past him, he noticed Mary's drawn face, and terrified expression, and decided to walk up to Mary's house to find out what was going on.

In spite of her age Mrs Smith was out of the trap, and waiting for Mary to open her front door before Mary's feet had reached the pavement. Following Mary through the house, the rather formidable widow found a startled Mary-Ann in the kitchen preparing the evening meal for the family. Assuming that Mrs Smith had come to talk to her mother, Mary-Ann wiped her hands on a towel and started to make her way up to her room.

Blocking her exit, Mrs Smith said, "Do not leave, young lady, because it is you that I have come to see. What is this I hear that you are not going to take the opportunity of going to University?"

Mary-Ann repeated once again the reasons for her decision, which were promptly dismissed by Mrs Smith, who said to Mary-Ann, "Don't be discouraged by a couple of set backs dear. What are you doing tomorrow morning?"

Somewhat indignantly Mary-Ann replied, "I'm going to look for a job."

"Oh no, you are not!" the widow informed her. "I shall meet you here at 9.30 tomorrow morning. I have made arrangements for us to meet your Headmistress, and we shall not be leaving her office until we have arranged an interview for you at a suitable university."

It was at this point that both David and William, who had met each other on the door step, burst through the door because they were concerned that Mary was in some form of trouble. Both were promptly ordered out of the room by the redoubtable Mrs Smith, who then turned to Mary-Ann, who like her mother appeared to be rather shell-shocked by the events that had happened during the last ten minutes, and simply said to her, "Well?"

Recovering quickly, Mary-Ann made her reply.

"Much as I appreciate your offer of help, I have already decided that it would be unfair to expect my mother to continue to support me for another eight years. I realise it is now time for me to help the rest of the family by contributing towards my upkeep."

There was silence in the room for a moment. Mary was about to say to her daughter that she was not worried about that, when Mrs Smith who until now had remained calm suddenly lost her temper, and said to Mary-Ann, "I have been looking for many years to find a way of making amends for the manner in which my son treated your mother, when he took over the business from my late husband. I knew that she would be too proud to accept what she considered to be charity, and now I have the opportunity to put right the wrong that was done by my family all those years ago. If I provide you with the money, Mary-Ann, I know that you will make much better use of it than my son, who will only waste any money that I leave to him when I die."

Looking at both of the women opposite her and seeing no form of dissent she concluded, "Thank you both for listening to me; I will pick up Mary-Ann at 9.30 tomorrow morning. Make sure that you are ready, young lady." She then turned, and swept past the two men who were still in the hallway where they were standing after they had been ejected from the kitchen a few minutes earlier.

Mary followed Mrs Smith out to her pony and trap, and on the pavement her former employer turned to her before she climbed into the trap, and said, "I don't want to hear another word, Mary. As soon as I realised at the meeting of the school governors who Miss Hopkins, the Headmistress, was talking about, I was determined to make amends for the wrong that was done so long ago. Please make an old lady very happy by allowing me to do so." Mary, realising that she was about to burst into tears once again, simply nodded and turned back into the house, as Mrs Smith climbed into the trap and set off down the road.

Returning to the kitchen, Mary faced a barrage of questions, from Mary-Ann. "Why is she doing this for me mum?"

From William, "What is going on?"

And from David, "Who was that? What did she want? Is everything alright?"

Finally she managed to answer all their questions, and after David had departed she cooked the evening meal that Mary-Ann had started. Mary sat up long after the washing up had been done, and the children had gone to bed, mulling over the events of that evening and wondering if she should accept Mrs Smith's offer, or if she could afford to pay the fees herself, although she had no idea how much they were likely to be. Finally she went to bed, and eventually managed to get to sleep.

The following day she had to leave for work before Mary-Ann was collected, and for the whole day Mary's mind was not on her job. She spent the time wondering what, if any, news there would be for her when she returned home. The journey that evening seemed to take much longer than usual, but when Mary eventually arrived home she found that a meal was on the table waiting for her. Pausing only to thank Mary-Ann for the lovely meal, Mary blurted out, "Well, what happened today?" and was rather taken aback when her daughter calmly replied, "Mum, we shall just have to wait and see."

A fortnight later, when she returned home from work in the evening, she was met at the door by a very excited Mary-Ann with an official-looking letter in her hand. As Mary came through the door she was hugged by her daughter who was both laughing and at the same time crying, as she told her mother that she had been invited to attend an interview at the Imperial College in London in ten days time.

Although Mary had never been to London before, that did not stop her from asking Mary-Ann if she wanted her to go up to London to help, when she attended the interview. Dejected when her daughter replied, with more confidence than she really felt, that she would be alright, Mary then became determined that she would see her daughter off from the station, when she left on the London-bound train on her special day.

Finally the big day came. After they arrived at Taunton, Mary had a quiet word with Jim, the guard that she had seen and spoken to on many mornings during the past ten years, while her daughter was out of earshot at the bookstall selecting a magazine for her trip.

When Mary had explained the situation, Jim agreed to speak to the Guard on the Paddington train who would then ensure that Mary-Ann did not experience any problems either during her journey, or on her arrival at Paddington. As the train pulled out of the station Mary-Ann noticed that her mother had only just been able to hold back her tears, and that now her eyes were filling, as she waved goodbye. At this moment Mary-Ann's self confidence was rapidly ebbing and the sight of her mother close to tears did nothing to improve the situation.

That evening David travelled on the train to Bishops Lydeard station on his own, while Mary drank numerous cups of tea as she waited for her daughter's train to arrive. As each train from London pulled into the platform she would rush out from the Refreshment Room to look for Mary-Ann's face amongst the passengers alighting from the train. Only after they had all left the platform, and there was still no sign of her daughter, would Mary return to the refreshment rooms for yet another cup of tea.

Finally at 8.05pm, the 4.20pm train from Paddington, arrived on time. The train was crowded, and many of the passengers were alighting at Taunton. Long before Mary spotted her daughter's face amongst the crowd, and she heard her excited voice calling out, "Mum, mum!"

When she was still some distance from her mother, she could not keep the news to herself any longer, and called out so loudly that many of the people on the platform, including Jim the guard, heard her.

"They have offered me a place!" and then she rushed into her mothers arms and embraced her, whispering as she did, so that no one else could hear, "Thank you, mum – for everything."

The pair continued to hug each other for so long in a silent embrace, that they would have missed the last train to Bishops Lydeard, but for Jim the Guard, who walked along the platform to within a few feet of them, quietly coughed, and then said, "Mrs Hawkes, do you want to catch the 8.15pm train? It is ready to leave now Ma'am."

Turning to Mary-Ann he said, "Congratulations, young lady, I shall miss your smiling face each day when you have gone to London."

On the way home from the station they both had to call at David's house to tell him what had happened, because he had asked them to. When he heard the news he insisted they should all go to the Lethbridge Arms for a celebratory drink. David himself did not drink, Mary did not frequent a pub very often, and for Mary-Ann it was the first time that she had ever been in the bar of a public house, and like the other two with her she had no idea of what to order.

"A little port and lemon will do you no harm," her mother assured her, so David ordered two port and lemons for the ladies and an orange juice for himself.

The landlord knew David, Mary and also her daughter, even though they were infrequent visitors to his bar, so he was rather surprised that they had all decided to visit his pub on this particular evening. As he served him, the landlord asked David, "So what's the special reason for this visit?" When David told him of Mary-Ann's success, he refused to accept payment for their drinks and informed him that the drinks were on the house. Before they left that evening, all the regulars in the bar were aware of Mary-Ann's achievements and were offering to buy her drinks. She was rather embarrassed when she had to keep saying to them, "Thank you very much, but I do not drink."

They left the pub that night much later than they had intended, after drinking an awful lot of lemonade and orange juice, none of which they had paid for. Mary only just managed to get some fish and chips for their much delayed evening meal before the shop closed.

When the day came for Mary-Ann to go up to the University, no matter how much her daughter protested, Mary insisted that she would take the day off work, and go up to London to help Mary-Ann with her luggage, and also ensure that the luggage sent in advance by train, had arrived safely. In reality, of course, Mary wanted to ensure that the rooms in the hall of residence were suitable for her daughter.

PERSONNEL MATTERS

After the departure of Mary-Ann the house was quiet. Mary missed her daughter's infectious laughter, and the meals that she often prepared, and had waiting on her arrival home from work. William was often out in the evening, or late home from work, and so she spent many long hours in the evening on her own, listening to the recently purchased 'wireless'. It was at moments like this that she sometimes wished she had accepted David's offer of marriage, but she realised it was too late now for her to change her mind. She also knew that, had she married David, she would been have forced to make a choice between marriage, and the career she was creating by her own efforts.

Mary, like others who embarked on the new career of Personnel Officer at that time, found the job was evolving as the months went by. At first, it seemed all that was required of her was that she should advertise for and interview applicants for the various vacancies within the company. If, during the interview, she decided that the candidate before her was suitable for the position, she would send the applicant to the manager of the department concerned. If he agreed with Mary's choice, they would then be engaged, and return to Mary's office before leaving the premises, so that she could familiarise them with the terms and conditions of their employment.

After a few months Mary found that she was also becoming involved in the welfare problems of many of the employees. Like most good ideas it started by accident when she found that one member of the shop floor staff had been absent from work for some weeks, recovering from an accident sustained on her way to work. Mary learned the circumstances of the accident when she visited the woman at home one day.

She had been knocked down and injured by a milk-float when the milkman's horse bolted having been frightened by a passing car that back-fired.

The absence of any company sick pay scheme, and with very little in the way of state benefits available, the woman was suffering severe financial hardship as a result. When Mary returned to her office she started to investigate the possibility of the woman's receiving some compensation from the milkman's Public Liability Insurance. In the meantime her friends on the shop floor arranged a collection for her and asked Mary if she would like to contribute, which she was happy to do.

After the collection had been made, Mary was approached to arrange for it to be delivered to their friend. Shortly before she left the office with the extremely generous gift of £10 from her colleagues, Mary contacted the solicitors for the Dairy Company's insurers, and was pleased to learn that they intended to make an interim payment, pending the full recovery of the accident victim. As Mary had not previously told the employee of the correspondence on her behalf, the unfortunate lady was delighted to learn of the impending change in her fortunes. When Mary said goodbye to her as she left after her visit, she noticed that the victim was looking much happier than when she had arrived.

When the lady concerned returned to work some weeks later after she had made a full recovery, she wasted no time in telling her companions on the shop floor of the action that Mary had taken on her behalf. As the news spread, it led to some rather unexpected developments. Soon Mary found that many of the employees in the offices, together with those on the factory floor were either stopping her as she walked around the premises, or coming to her office. They wanted to inform her of friends or relations who wanted to work for the company, and before long she had a waiting list of people who wished to join the firm. Others told her of any staff they suspected of wrong doing, which they considered would reflect on the remainder of the employees.

A manager used an expletive when he thought no one was around, but unfortunately it was overheard by a member of the staff, who also sang in the local church choir. Upset at what she had heard, she handed in her notice to Mary who then attempted to find out the reasons for her impending departure. She established that the lady in question did not want the manager to be dismissed, saying she was certain he had not realised he could be overheard, and knew that he did not usually use bad language. Mary went to the Manager concerned, and without revealing the identity of the complainant, informed him of the problem he had inadvertently caused. He could not even recall the incident, but immediately apologised, and asked Mary to convey his apologies to the person concerned, for what he assured Mary was an isolated and unpardonable lapse. Satisfied at the outcome, the services of another valued employee were retained.

As a result of this occurrence it became company policy that all managers were to tackle minor welfare incidents immediately they arose, simply to ensure that they did not become major problems. If managers felt that they could not deal with the matter themselves, they were instructed to refer it to Mary, who was expected to resolve it with the minimum of delay.

Such a dialogue had not been heard of in the factory in the past, but once the routine became established, it was noticeable that production levels throughout the company rose, although staffing levels remained constant. Staff turnover rates were reduced, leading to lower training costs, and higher skill levels amongst the remainder of the staff. In turn this resulted in lower reject levels and production costs, and reduced union activity amongst the employees. These improvements led to an enlightened management team, and happier staff.

When Mary-Ann was at home at the end of her second year at University, she learned of the death of her benefactor, Mrs Smith. Although neither Mary nor her daughter had been invited to attend the funeral service, they both went to the church, sitting at the back of the congregation, as far away from her former employer's son as possible. Walking away from the graveside after the service Mary heard that a number of people had been invited to the reading of the will, and she wondered if the trust fund set up for Mary-Ann's education would be affected by Mrs Smith's demise.

A week later Mary received a letter from the solicitor handling her former employer's affairs, and learned that she was a beneficiary. However, Mrs Smith had insisted that she did not attend the reading of the will, because she feared that her son might cause some unpleasantness when he learned of its contents. The solicitor then went on to inform Mary that he had been instructed to administer the trust fund which had been set up for Mary-Ann's education. He also asked if she would have any objections if, to avoid unnecessary delays, he asked Mary-Ann to deal with him when she needed any funds from the trust. Mary's relief at this news quickly turned to shock when she read, in the final paragraph of the letter, that her former employer had also left her a small bequest of £500, in appreciation of the help that Bill and Mary had given to her all those years ago.

With the money that William was providing to cover his housekeeping, together with her own salary, Mary could think of nothing that she needed immediately, except possibly a new coat for the winter, so she decided to open a Post Office Savings Account, in case she needed the money for a rainy day.

Mary was relieved that William seemed to be happy and contented with his life, now that he was driving the new lorries full time. One of his regular trips involved collecting new wagons and carts from the factory at the far end of the village, and delivering them to various farmers and companies throughout Somerset, Dorset and Devon, sometimes travelling as far afield as Gloucester. After he had been driving the lorries for about twelve months he found himself working longer hours than ever before. Then the company he was working for won a contract to carry out much of the site preparation and haulage work on the new anti-aircraft gunnery training site that was being built at Doniford Bay.

When the site had first been established about ten years earlier it had been used by members of the Territorial Army during their Summer camps, and the TA soldiers had been billeted under canvas. In the 1930s it was decided that the site would become a permanent camp, with gunnery platforms, blast bays, magazines (to store the ammunition), and wooden huts to billet the permanent garrison, the trainee gunners and their instructors. The guardroom and officers' mess, offices and married quarters (built a short distance away from the main camp) were also included in the contract.

The bulk of the materials required for this work, including hard core, timber, bricks, slates, all internal fittings, tarmac and cement, came from outside the area mainly by rail, to the sidings at either Williton or Watchet to be unloaded, and then taken by road to the site. Some materials were routed through the docks at Watchet and were also forwarded to the site by road. On many days William found himself making four, or sometimes five trips between Williton or Watchet and Doniford. William was also expected to help load and unload the lorry, so often when he arrived home in the evenings he was so tired he would eat his evening meal and then go straight to bed.

Some of the timber that was used on the project was obtained from local sources. William looked forward to these trips, because if it came from the sawmills at Simonsbath, it meant that only one round trip could be completed in a day. Trips to and from the sawmills at Dunster were almost as welcome, because only two round trips could be completed. William had already learned that it was easier to drive the lorry, than be continually loading and unloading it.

Mary always knew when her son had been driving his lorry for most of the time, because when he came home in the evening he washed and changed, and after he had finished his meal, he would wander down to the pub for a well-earned pint of cider. On other evenings when he had finished a day of short trips, after he had finished his evening meal, he would often slump in his chair in the sitting room, listening with his mother to 'Geraldo and his Orchestra' on the wireless for a short time, before he fell asleep in the chair.

Mary was pleased that whenever her daughter had a long break from her studies she would return home. Although Mary did not approve of the makeup and lipstick her daughter was now using, she was relieved to see that she was not wearing some of the outrageous London 'flapper' fashions that appeared in the newspapers. What Mary-Ann found touching, but at the same time rather wearing, was her mother's constant worrying about her health. Whenever she arrived home one of the first questions her mother asked was, "Are you eating enough, dear? Are you sure that you are all right? You do look rather thin, you're not studying too hard are you?"

Whenever the opportunity arose, Mary-Ann would cook and serve the meals for the family when she was at home, not simply because she wished to help her mother, but she knew that if her mother cooked for the family, she would insist on serving large portions to her daughter, who she remained convinced was losing weight and was rather thin. What Mary did not know, was that her daughter was very conscious of her figure, and kept to a strict diet, and exercise regime during term time. She often lost between seven and ten pounds, only to find when she returned to University after a spell of her mother's home cooking, she had regained all the weight previously lost, and had to start again.

Another concern of Mary's was that all the time she was at home, her daughter would continue to study every day, sometimes throughout the whole day and often late into the night. She did not appear to take any time off to relax. Whenever Mary spoke to Mary-Ann on the subject, she was assured by her daughter that she would not make herself ill through overwork. These reassurances were of little benefit to Mary, who continued to worry about her daughter.

PEACEFUL TIMES

In 1938 Mary-Ann passed her finals and became a qualified Doctor. Although she checked every edition of the British Medical Journal for a post as a General Practitioner, she also obtained temporary work in the Casualty and Accident department of the London Hospital in the Mile End Road between Whitechapel and Bow, in the East End of London.

Working in this area came as a complete culture shock to Mary-Ann. Nothing that she had experienced previously in her life had prepared her for the squalor and deprivation that most of her patients lived in. Many of those who visited the hospital were dressed in rags and had only recently settled in the area. They were often immigrants, mainly Jewish, who had fled from Eastern Europe or Russia, who were now being joined by an increasing number of refugees from Nazi Germany. Overcrowding in the slums of the area was rife, and tuberculosis, and other infectious diseases were common. The situation stood little chance of improving while many of the local people could not afford even the most basic medical care, and minor symptoms were often neglected until they became life threatening before relatives of the patient sought and received treatment for them.

During the time she was working at the hospital Mary-Ann wrote trying to obtain interviews for the many General Practitioner vacancies advertised in the British Medical Journal. A large number of her early applications were simply ignored, and so later she put only her initials on her application. At first this ploy was successful and she obtained a number of interviews, but she soon began to recognise the look of utter incredulity on the (male) doctor's face when a woman appeared for the interview.

After she had been asked to sit down there usually followed several irrelevant questions, while the interviewer frantically thought of a reason to get Mary-Ann out of the room as soon as he possibly could.

During this dark period in her life, when it seemed to her that she would never be able to obtain the position that she wanted, she was encouraged by the attitude of a large number of the immigrants she came into contact with. Many of these people had finished up working in the rag trade for a pittance, but were convinced that one day they would be running their own businesses, and that they would become wealthy.

Many of them could not afford medical treatment but would always insist on making some form of payment in kind. Often Mary-Ann would be given a grubby piece of paper with a name and address written on it, after she had finished treating one of her patients, and would be told that if she contacted their Uncle / Cousin / Father / Brother (in-law) etc., they would do her 'a very good deal', at the right price on a suit / blouse / dress, / skirt, - "All good *schmutter**, just mention my name."

At first Mary-Ann ignored these offers until one day she met by accident one of her former patients as she was doing her shopping in the Mile End Road. In response to her enquiry about his health, she learned that not only had he recovered from his illness (he had been admitted to hospital suffering from pneumonia) but also that she had inadvertently offended him. She learned the reason he was offended was because she had not taken advantage of the offer he had made to her when he left hospital, that she should visit his brother who would make something nice for her to wear. He continued, "My brother, he is a very good tailor, the very best in the area; all his suits are of the very finest material, and if you do not visit him he will be offended, because he will believe that you think that his clothes are not good enough for you."

Anxious to avoid giving any further offence, she assured her former patient that she would visit his brother on the next day that she had off from work. At this time most of the High Street shops in the country were closed and the streets deserted on a Sunday. Because so many of the shops and stalls in the East End were owned and staffed by Jewish people, the whole area was bustling with activity on the Sunday when she made her way to the address that she had been given, which was just off Middlesex Street, more often known as Petticoat Lane.

When she finally found the premises, she entered the dimly lit shop and asked for Mr Cohen. As soon as she had established her identity, she was greeted as if she had been a customer of his for many years.

"What would you like, my dear?" he said. Rather embarrassed, and still uncertain whether they had expected her to take up the offer that had been made, she answered nervously, "Could I have a blouse, would that be possible please?" Her request was promptly dismissed, and she was informed that, "A nice lady like you, my dear, should have a smart suit." Her concerns over the cost were brushed aside, and immediately a lady, who Mary-Ann assumed was his wife, appeared from a room at the back of the shop, and proceeded to take her measurements. She was then invited to examine a cluster of materials and various patterns, before she finally selected a dark grey pinstripe cloth and a suitable business pattern. She was then informed that if she called back in seven days time, a made-to-measure grey pinstripe suit consisting of a skirt and jacket would be ready for her to collect.

When she returned to the shop the following week, she found that not only was the suit ready, but when she tried it on in the changing room at the back, it fitted perfectly. Returning to the front of the shop with the suit over her arm, she had to assure Mr Cohen ("Call me Solly, my dear,") several times that the suit was perfect; furthermore it was just what she wanted, and it fitted her like a glove. Only then did Solly carefully wrap it in layers of white tissue paper, then in brown paper before tying up the parcel with string. Still worried that she would not be able to afford to pay for the suit she nervously asked Mr Cohen how much she owed him, and was informed that her made-to-measure suit would cost her ten bob (50p) and that he very much hoped that he would have the pleasure of serving her again.

After this experience Mary-Ann spent many of the days when she was not on duty in the hospital, wandering around Petticoat Lane, and the surrounding streets in search of bargains. Sometimes she wondered if her bargains had 'fallen off the back of a lorry', and these, together with offers of assistance from many of her grateful patients soon ensured that she had a well-stocked wardrobe.

By now, whenever she sent off an application for a job, Mary-Ann ensured that the potential interviewer was aware of her gender. She found that this tactic avoided wasting both her own time, and that of the interviewer. It also ensured that she did not incur any unnecessary travelling expenses. Unfortunately it often meant that she did not receive any reply at all, and if she did, it was usually to inform her that the position had been filled.

After many frustrating months, she could hardly believe her eyes when she opened a letter one morning from a Dr. McAndrew who had written from an address in Chadwell Heath, asking her to attend an interview on Thursday of the following week. After checking to make sure that the letter had not been sent to her in error, (it had not), her next task was to find the whereabouts of this place called Chadwell Heath. Eventually she found that it was in Essex (just), on the outskirts of East London. As soon as she had made arrangements with one of her colleagues to cover for her in her absence, she wrote back to confirm that she would be able to keep the appointment.

A week later, early on the Thursday morning, she caught a train from Liverpool Street Station that she hoped would arrive in time to ensure that she would not be late for her appointment at 11.30am. During her journey as she sat looking out of the grimy windows of the railway carriage, she noticed that many of the slum dwellings she was passing were so close to the railway line that she could look straight into their tiny windows: the outside 'privies' belonging to these houses almost formed part of the railway embankment. She also noticed as she passed by, that from the amount of smoke coming over the top of the doors in a number of the privies that many were occupied at that moment. She wondered what, if any, reaction there was from the occupants, as the train thundered by just a few feet from them. At the same time her nostrils were assailed by the bouquet of smells that arose from the various factories alongside the railway line, from the pungent smell of the Bryant & May match factory at Bow, to the heady smell of the Yardley scent factory at Stratford.

After the train had passed through Ilford the scenery started to become a little more rural in appearance and the train stopped at stations called Seven Kings, and Goodmayes. Eventually it arrived at a station which the porter on the platform announced was 'Chad'll 'Eaf' which she surmised correctly was her destination. Having climbed the steps from the platform, as she made her way along the passage at the top of the stairs to the exit she was enveloped in a cloud of steam from the departing engine, which had came up through the gaps in the floorboards. Staggering through the temporary fog she almost bumped into the small man standing outside his box, collecting tickets from the few passengers who had alighted from the train.

After apologising to him, she then asked, "Could you tell me the way to Chadwell Heath Lane?"

After a slight pause he said, "Turn left, down the 'ill, bear right at the bottom and when yer gets to the copper shop, it's orposit." Relieved to learn that the English Language was being murdered as successfully in Essex, as it was in the East End of London, she set off down the hill, which in reality was only the slope down from the road bridge that crossed the railway line. As she walked along she saw a large building on her left that was nearing completion, which she learned from the large sign at the front, was to be a new bakery for Hemmings the Master Bakers.

Reaching the bottom of the slope, she took the right hand fork and noticed evidence of more building work being carried out. On the corner of the two roads, there was a parade of shops of which a number had been completed, and some had been let. In the road to the left there was a large plot of land, that was still waiting to be developed. She then realised that she was approaching the police station, from the barking of the stray dogs that, against their will, had been incarcerated in the kennels. Arriving at the main road by the police station, she stood on the kerb for a moment, waiting for an approaching tram to pass, before crossing the road, and was rather embarrassed when the tram came to a halt at the terminus, some fifty yards before it reached her.

Feeling rather foolish, and hoping that no one else had noticed, she crossed the road and saw more new buildings as she did so. A newly built block of shops and flats, all of which appeared to be occupied; a new cinema, the Gaumont, further along the main road; the new bank building on one corner of the cross-roads, and on the opposite corner a newly built public house, The Coopers Arms. Walking up the lane she noticed how clean the area looked, compared with the East End of London where she had been living for the past few months. It also struck her as rather odd that there was such a mixture of suburbia, light industry and, as she was to find out later at the far end of the lane, open countryside, all in the length of the mile long road.

Anxious to make a good impression by arriving on time, or perhaps a couple of minutes early for her interview, she started to walk briskly along the lane. She noticed that the first premises she passed was a builder's merchants with a large selection of materials lying in the yard next to the road without a fence to prevent anyone taking the materials on view. As she passed she wondered how much stock they lost each night – none, she later discovered.

Next door to the builder's yard was a large Victorian detached house, with extensive lawns both to the front and the rear of the house that were beautifully trimmed and edged. The outstanding feature of the house was a enormous flag pole with the Union Jack fluttering at the top, which stood outside the front door, and the occupant of the house insisted that the flag was raised at 9am every morning, and was lowered every evening at dusk.

Alongside this house was a large open area that obviously belonged to the local allotment holders association, with all the plots carefully tended. This was followed by a mixture of late Victorian, and Edwardian houses, while on the opposite side of the road was a continuous development of houses and flats that had only recently been built. More new houses had been constructed in the side roads that had been laid out, from the lane. After a further half a mile there was a block of shops, again on the opposite side of the road, followed by a plot of undeveloped land between the end shop and the next building, which was an Off Licence that stood on the corner of Roxy Avenue. On the side of the road she was walking along there was another block of shops, at the end of which, on the corner of Percy Road, was a chemist shop and pharmacy, which she thought was rather convenient because it was opposite the doctor's surgery she was looking for.

The house the Doctor lived in was at the end of a block of terraced houses that had been built on the main road in the last few years. For the benefit of his patients, or possibly to preserve his own living space, the doctor had built a single storey extension at the back of the house in what had originally been the back garden. The door to the waiting room was in the side road at the end of the extension furthest from the house. Finding the door open, she walked into the waiting room and found that it occupied only part of the extension, the remainder of the area being the Doctor's consulting room. Next to the door leading into that room was a bell push together with a notice that read: 'Please ring for attention.'

Having rung the bell, she was about to sit down on one of what appeared to be the very comfortable chairs in the waiting room, when the door suddenly opened. A short wizened little man appeared, whose hair, or rather what was left of it, was now mainly grey but had once been ginger. He opened the door and in a broad Scottish accent, that thirty years spent in England had done little to diminish, invited her in.

He took her through the consulting room into the sitting room of the house, and after inviting her to sit down, informed her that she must need a nice cup of tea after her long journey. Without waiting for her reply he dashed out, to reappear shortly afterwards with a tray that was carefully laid out with a Royal Dalton china tea pot, sugar bowl, milk jug, and two cups and saucers. As Mary-Ann sat drinking her tea Dr Alistair McAndrew was reading her CV. He then explained, that, as she had already guessed, the large number of houses which had recently been built in the area had resulted in a corresponding increase in the number of patients registered with him. She found herself wondering why he had left it for so long before advertising for some assistance, when for the first of what was to be many occasions he appeared to read her mind. He explained that he had been trying for some time to get an assistant, but all the applicants he had seen to date, who had all been male, seemed to regard the area as the last outpost of the Empire, being neither City nor truly rural.

He then went on to describe how he had tried to cope with his extra workload.

"I did purchase a small car, but that has proved to be of little use because the damn thing keeps breaking down!" Suddenly he paused for a moment and said to her, "Can you drive a car, young lady?"

When she informed him that she could, he announced, "Well if you decide to join the practise you may have the car, and I will go back to my trusty pony and trap." At that moment she was rather concerned what her potential patients would think if she was late for an appointment, because of the unreliability of the car, but she was to learn that the cause of its frequent failures, was not the fault of the vehicle itself, but the driver.

It appeared that, although he was an extremely competent doctor, he had no idea of how to operate anything that was remotely mechanical. He would climb into his car and drive off each day, never bothering to fill it with petrol, with the result that it would eventually come to a standstill, normally at the furthest point on his rounds from the surgery. He would then jump out of the car to finish off his rounds on foot. When he returned to the surgery, he would pick up the telephone, and when the poor unfortunate woman at the local telephone exchange answered, he would bellow down the phone, "Get me that damn rogue at the garage," adding as an afterthought, "Please." Because it was such a regular occurrence, eventually all the operators on the exchange knew to whom he was referring, and promptly put him through to Greens Garage.

When Les the garage proprietor answered the phone, and heard the broad Scottish voice ranting at the other end of the line, he would wait until the tirade ended, and would then ask where the Doctor had left his car. He then set off to recover it, picking up the full jerry can of petrol that he kept for these emergencies and either walked out to the stranded car, or he got a lift on the pillion of his apprentice's motorbike. Having emptied the contents of the can into the tank of the car, he would drive it back to the garage and fill the car's petrol tank to the brim, from the hand-operated petrol pump that stood in the forecourt of the garage, before returning it to the Doctor's surgery. Handing over the car keys Les would inform the Doctor, yet again, "S'alright now," before reminding him that, "the car would go a lot better if you filled it with petrol from time to time; always remember to look at the petrol gauge." He had said this to the Doctor on many occasions in the past, and each time had received the same reply "Ach, yes, all right," whereupon the Doctor promptly forgot the warning. For his part the Doctor could never understand how Les was able to locate the fault so quickly, every time, and assumed that it was all part of a dark plot to swell the garage owner's profits.

After he had offered the car to Mary-Ann the Doctor continued, "I think that I can say that if you join the practise you will be accepted by two thirds of my patients. The women and children will accept you, of course, but some of the more elderly male patients may be less willing to do so, and I think it best if I continue to deal with some of them. The only other group that you will have to worry about are the drunks, and they will be in no position to argue anyway!" This last remark was a reference to the fact that she would be expected to attend the local Police Station, usually on Friday or Saturday nights to confirm that some of their temporary guests were 'drunk and disorderly' within the meaning of the law.

Mary-Ann replied with a smile. "I've already encountered a great deal of prejudice from some patients, and feel that I am now able to cope with it." She then received a mild rebuke from the Doctor, when he said, "Aye, lass, I have no doubt that you have, but there is no reason why you have to face it, when you don't need to."

Before bringing the interview to an end, he told her that if she did decide to join the practice, he would be delighted to have her as a partner. As she said goodbye to him, before leaving, she promised that she would think over his proposals, and would let him know of her decision as soon as possible.

Leaving the surgery she walked back down the lane deep in thought, and suddenly found herself in the High Street. Out of the corner of her eye she saw a large model of a modern house, in the side window of the offices of Ashtons the Estate Agents, on the corner of the High Street and Chadwell Heath Lane. She walked over to the window to take a closer look at the detailed model, and noticed a sign in the window announcing that she could rent a modern three bedroomed house like that, for eight shillings and sixpence per week (42.5p).

Intrigued, she entered the shop and was welcomed by a little man of about fifty years old. He appeared not only to be asthmatic, but also a heavy smoker to judge by his nicotine-stained fingers, and the amount of cigarette ash down the front of the waistcoat of his rather worn blue suit. Finally she noticed that his hair appeared to be dyed black, was Brylcreemed* and combed straight back.

After Mary-Ann had informed him of her needs, he advised her that they had several houses to let, but the one he thought that she would prefer to see was in Reynolds Avenue. When Mary-Ann asked for directions, he informed her that it was only about half a mile away, and that he would be delighted to take her to the house immediately, and show her around it. After she agreed to his suggestion, he picked up his cigarettes and lighter, and as they went out, he turned round a sign on the back of the door to read: 'Closed - back in thirty minutes', and locked the premises as he left.

Mary-Ann found herself once again walking back up the same lane, but this time on the opposite side of the road, finally turning left down a side road, about two hundred yards before they reached the surgery. It was a long avenue, lined with small blocks of modern terraced houses that were about fifteen years old, on both sides of the road. The house in question was an end of terrace house, about halfway down the road on the right hand side. After Mr Reeves, from the Estate Agents, had opened the front door to let her in, he waited in the hall while Mary-Ann wandered around the house. She liked the sitting room with the large bow fronted window, the separate dining room with French windows leading out into the garden, and a modern kitchen, complete with larder. Upstairs there were three bedrooms, the smallest of which she decided to use as an office, together with a bathroom, and separate toilet. Unable to believe her luck, she asked Mr Reeves if she could continue to look round the house for a short while, and then lock up and return the keys to his office shortly. This request he readily agreed to.

After Mr Reeves had left, Mary-Ann unlocked the French windows, and went out into the long but rather narrow back garden. Down the centre of it there was a concrete path, flanked on both sides by lawns that now needed trimming, with well-stocked flower beds between the edge of the lawn and the wooden boundary fence on each side of the garden. She sat on a small seat in the shade of a small apple tree, for a while listening to the birds singing, noticing how peaceful the area seemed. It was not long before she made up her mind to accept both the job offer, and the tenancy of the house, before any one else had the chance to do so. Returning to the house she locked the French windows, and after looking around the house once more, reluctantly closed and locked the front door. She started to walk back up the road with the intention of going straight to the Estate Agents, but at the top of the road she changed her mind, and made her way to the surgery instead.

After she rang the bell in the waiting room for the second time that day, a rather surprised Dr. McAndrew appeared, and seemed genuinely pleased when she announced that she had already made up her mind, and would like to accept his offer. The doctor asked the reason she had made up her mind so quickly. Mary-Ann then told him of her experience at the Estate Agents, and after a momentary pause the doctor replied, "Aye, that will be Mr Reeves of Ashtons that you saw, and as you will have no doubt observed he suffers badly from asthma. Mind you, his smoking doesn't help; perhaps you will be able to persuade him to stop, I have not been able to." In response to the Doctor's next enquiry Mary-Ann informed him that she hoped to be able to start at the beginning of next month, where upon he shook her hand warmly, and then asked her, "You must let me know as soon as you are able to confirm your starting date."

Returning to the Estate Agents she told Mr Reeves that she would like to lease the property as soon as possible, and she blushed when he said to her, "I understand that you are the new doctor." He then added, "I think that you might have some problems working out the blood pressure, and pulse rate of some of the younger men in the area, when you examine them. But to be serious for a moment I would like to be the very first person to welcome you to the area, and to congratulate you on your appointment."

After she had signed the necessary documents, and had said goodbye to Mr Reeves, she started to make her way to the station, suddenly realising that, to judge from her experiences on the first day, the area had a very effective 'bush telegraph' system. If Mr Reeves was anything to go by the inhabitants also appeared to have a rather wicked sense of humour. As Mary-Ann sat in the train on her way back to Liverpool Street station, she began to think of the numerous tasks she would need to undertake during the next four weeks. The first thing was to notify her mother of her success. At first she thought of sending her a telegram, but she then remembered how upset her mother became whenever she saw a telegram boy approaching the house. She decided that as soon as she got back to the nursing home she would write a letter to her mother and try to get it in the post that night so that she would receive it the following morning.

The following day when she returned to the hospital she notified the registrar, in writing, that she wished to leave the hospital at the end of the month. When her colleagues learned of the reason for her departure all her women colleagues, and some of the men she worked with, offered her their congratulations. The news of her impending departure spread like wildfire amongst her patients, and ex-patients, and before long she was being stopped both in the hospital, and the street by them, and many of their relatives that she had met on the wards, to say how sorry they were to learn that she was leaving.

Three days later Mary-Ann received a letter from her mother saying how thrilled she was that Mary-Ann had achieved her ambition. At the same time she informed her daughter that she had made arrangements to take a week's holiday and would be arriving in London on Saturday 8th to make certain that every thing was all right in her new house and that there was nothing that she needed. She also learned that her mother would be catching the 12.13pm train from Bishops Lydeard, which was due into London at 4.05pm, and would Mary-Ann please meet her mother at Paddington station. Mary-Ann wrote back to confirm the arrangements and at the same time enquire about William's welfare during the time her mother was away, only to be reminded in a letter she received two days later that her brother was old enough to look after himself for a week; "It will do him good," she said.

SETTLING TIMES

When some people heard that she was moving into a house, she was often invited to go with them to one of the many second hand furniture shops in the area. Each time the dialogue was the same: "Hymie, (or Solly, etc.) the doctor is leaving the area and setting up house, and she needs a good bed / table / set of chairs / wardrobe etc., can you do her a special deal?" Once she had acquired most of the furniture the next problem was how to get it to her house. There were of course plenty of volunteers, but none of them could travel as far as Chadwell Heath on the Sabbath, and she thought that her new neighbours and patients would not approve if she arrived at her new house, with all her furniture, on a Sunday.

Eventually a compromise was reached and two Gentiles who were friends of friends, were coerced into doing the job on a Saturday. When the removal day came, she was relieved that it was not raining because a flat bed lorry arrived which, like the driver and his mate, smelled strongly of fish. All her precious furniture was loaded onto the lorry and secured with what appeared to be a not very thick piece of rope, with many knots in it. Once the driver and his mate had checked once again that the load was secure, she was invited to jump up into the cab, and she found herself perched on the cover over the engine of the lorry, between the driver and his mate.

They set off through the East End, and Mary-Ann was convinced that they had taken a wrong turning in Stratford Broadway when they turned left, after she had seen a signpost pointing to the right for Ilford. In spite of her protests they assured her that they knew the way, and before long she was travelling through places she had never heard of. When they passed a large public house called the Green Man she was informed that they were at Leytonstone, after that Wanstead, and shortly afterwards the driver turned, and solemnly informed her that, "This is Gants 'ill and this is where Solly has just moved to, 'e's doing all right for 'isself."

Delighted as she was to learn of Solly's good fortune, of more immediate concern to Mary-Ann was the effect that the now rather warm engine cover was having on her bottom.

Soon she spotted another Green Man public house, but before she could ask if they were going round in circles, her head came into violent contact with the cab roof as they went far too quickly over a narrow hump-backed railway bridge. She immediately turned and glancing through the small window in the back of the cab was relieved to see that all her furniture still appeared to be on the back of the lorry.

Mary-Ann checked that her head was not cut, then became aware of a rapidly growing bump on the top of her head. Having regained her composure, she found they were travelling along a dual carriageway with modern houses on both sides of the road, in the type of ribbon development that was common in the 1930s. Entering an area of open countryside she noticed alongside the road a wooden site office on which a sign had been fixed informing prospective buyers that the new houses being built on that site could be purchased for £235 each.

Suddenly they were slowing down for a roundabout, and without anything to hold on to she almost finished up on the lap of the driver's mate, as they turned right without any warning, but before she could recover she was almost on the driver's lap as he then turned sharp left.

"'Ere we are," announced the driver. "Chad'ell 'eaf Lane." There must be some mistake, Mary-Ann thought, this cannot be the same road. They were still passing through open countryside with only the occasional house alongside the road. Half a mile further on they started to enter a more built up area with houses to her left, and a long brick wall on the opposite side. From the cab of the lorry she found she could see over the top of the wall, and was surprised to see a row of garages with a number of ambulances lined up outside. In answer to her question she was informed that it was the 'Isolation 'orspital'. In quick succession they passed a small recreation ground, several factories, and a number of almost new houses. At the very last moment she saw Dr. McAndrew's surgery and was able to shout at the driver, "turn right at the next turning, by the grocer's shop."

When the lorry pulled up outside the house, and she was able to get off the very warm engine cover she appreciated for the first time the sort of discomfort that her haemorrhoid patients experienced. Climbing down from the lorry she was met by Mr Reeves, who came out of the house to greet her, for he had been sitting on the stairs waiting for her. Handing over the keys of the house, he informed her, "The Gas Light and Coke Company man has delivered and installed the cooker for you, and if there are any problems would you please contact me immediately."

After Mary-Ann had thanked him, he touched his hat, and then started to walk back to his office, pausing after a few steps to light another of the many cigarettes that he would smoke that day.

On hearing that the cooker was in working order, the driver informed Mary-Ann that a cup of 'rosy' (Rosy Lea, Cockney rhyming slang for tea) "would be luverly." As she looked round the kitchen for something to boil the water in, and to try to find the tea, she heard a voice calling "Coooeeeee". When she opened the door to the hallway, there was a plump grey-haired lady standing there who informed her, "fort you would like a cup o' tea after your journey luv." She then placed on the working surface in the kitchen a tray containing three cups, all of which Mary-Ann noticed were marked LNER, together with a half empty bottle of milk, a blue paper packet containing some sugar, and a single teaspoon. Before departing she informed Mary-Ann that her name was Edith although everyone called her Edie and, "If you want anyfing else I'm only next door so just give me a shout." As she did not say which side she lived, Mary-Ann experienced some difficulty when the time came to return the contents of the tray.

After they had drunk their cups of tea the driver and his mate quickly unloaded the contents of the lorry and placed all the furniture in the house, in the positions selected by Mary-Ann. When they had finished unloading the lorry and had drunk their last cup of tea, she asked them how much she owed them, only to be informed that they had already been paid. She then offered them money for a drink (in other words, a tip) for all their hard work, and they politely refused her offer informing her that, "If Ikey found out that we took money from the lady doctor 'e would kill us." As she went to the door to see them off, the driver turned to her and said, "These geezers are lucky to have someone like you to look after them luv, I 'ope they appreciate it; if they don't you can allus come back to us." With that he turned on his heels, climbed up into the cab with his mate and drove off, leaving Mary-Ann feeling very emotional on the door step, as she suddenly realised just how many friends she had made in the short time she had spent in the East End of London.

The following day, Sunday, some of her friends from the hospital brought her personal belongings including her books, medical equipment, and clothes, in a van which for the remaining six days of the week delivered laundry to the hospital. To show her gratitude she was able to cook her first meal in the new house for her guests, before they departed. As Mary-Ann stood in the kitchen doing the washing up after they had left she suddenly realised that she had not discovered how they had managed to acquire the van, but she decided after some thought, that if you knew a friend, who knew a friend, you could obtain almost anything in the East End.

The following morning Mary-Ann reported to the surgery bright and early, and Dr McAndrew promptly handed her the keys to the car, a list of the patients she was expected to see, and a map of the area. When she got in the car she noticed to her horror that the petrol tank was almost empty, so she drove slowly to the local garage to fill the car. When Les, the owner of the establishment, saw the car arrive on the forecourt he could not believe his eyes, and promptly went out to investigate, thinking that it must have been stolen.

At first Mary-Ann could not understand why she was being treated with such suspicion, and why Les was reluctant to serve her. Then she saw a look of enlightenment cross his face as he exclaimed, "You must be the new lady doctor. 'As 'e given you 'is car then?" Only after she had confirmed that he had indeed done so, did he inform her of the reason for the frequent failures of the car in the past, (as already recounted), before filling up the car and allowing her to go on her way.

Although many of her patients shared a similar background to those she had met in the East End, and they were certainly not wealthy, there seemed to be no problem when it came to paying their doctor's bills. When she mentioned this to Doctor McAndrew he simply smiled and said, "That's the benefit of the H.S.A. (Hospital Savings Account) my dear." As she still looked puzzled, he explained, "By paying 2d (less than one new penny) a week for each member of the family, they are covered for most of their doctor's fees, and hospital expenses." Finally he told her, "Why don't you pop in to see Mr Hall, at his house on the corner of your road one Saturday morning, when most of his members come along to pay their weekly dues, then you can see how it works."

When she did visit Mr Hall a few weeks later she found a long queue of people that started by his front gate, and stretched round to the back of his house, and into the conservatory where Mr Hall sat collecting the money.

When Saturday 8th arrived, Mary-Ann completed her morning rounds as soon as possible, and not daring to take the car to Paddington in case she got lost, caught the train, arriving in plenty of time to ensure that her mother did not have to wait for her. After they had met and they were travelling back in the train from Liverpool Street, Mary kept exclaiming to her daughter, "How could you live in a place like this?" In spite of her daughter's assurances that where she was living was nothing like this part of London, it did not stop her mother making the same observation every five minutes throughout most of the journey.

When they arrived at her house, her mother spent a long time on the door step, looking up and down the road, noting which houses had freshly cleaned curtains and windows, and carefully tended front gardens. Eventually she went indoors to start her tour of inspection of the house, while Mary-Ann made them both a cup of tea. Although Mary-Ann had known this would happen, and had spent half the previous night cleaning and polishing the whole house, she was dreading the outcome of her Mother's inspection.

When, having completed the tour of the house, her Mother went through the kitchen, and out into the garden, without saying a word, Mary-Ann feared the worst. Finally she could stand the tension no longer and followed her mother into the garden to hand her a cup of tea, and noticed that she appeared to be deep in thought. When she heard her daughter's footsteps approaching Mary looked around and said to her, "The lawn needs cutting, have you got a lawnmower, dear?" On learning that she had not, Mary made a mental note of yet another thing she could get for her daughter's new house.

After they had eaten the evening meal Mary had prepared, and had done the washing up together, Mary-Ann took her mother for a walk round the neighbourhood, pointing out the surgery where she worked. From there they went to the local park and sat for a while watching the children playing on the swings and slide, and in the sand pit. Some of the children recognised Mary-Ann as their new doctor and said, "Hello." When dusk started to fall Mary-Ann and her mother, together with the many children in the park, started to make their way home, before the gates were locked for the night.

The following day, a Sunday, Mary-Ann attended the morning church service with her mother at St Paul's Church in Goodmayes and when the service had ended, introduced her mother to the vicar, the Reverend Smith. They left the church and drove up the lane to Little Heath. Then they crossed the Eastern Avenue and continued up Hainault Road until they reached the T junction at the top. There they turned right and after a short distance parked the car at the side of the road, near the foot of Hogg Hill. It was a beautiful sunny day and it was starting to get very warm, as they collected from the car the picnic Mary-Ann had prepared. After climbing over a stile they strolled along a footpath until they were halfway up the hill.

Finding a shady spot they spread out the blanket, and sat on it for a while looking across the countryside towards the smoky metropolis in the distance, while they listened to the buzzing of the bees, and the birds singing. Half a mile away some rather ancient biplanes practised circuits and bumps in a nearby field. Mary sat for a long time after they had finished their picnic, deep in thought, realising, that although the countryside was so different, she found herself recalling the times, long ago, when she and Bill, together with the children had spent similar days picnicking in the Quantock Hills. Neither Mary nor her daughter realised as they walked back to the car later, that in two year's time this peaceful scene would be shattered as men fought and died in the skies above this very spot during the Battle of Britain. Amongst their numbers would be some of the men they had just watched learning to fly the biplanes earlier in the nearby field.

The following day, while her daughter coped with the surgery and her house calls, Mary set off for the local shops armed with a list of items she wanted to get for her daughter's new house, after she had withdrawn the money from the local Post Office. On her way to the Post Office, Mary remembered the conditions attached to the bequest by Mrs Smith, but eased her conscience by claiming that she was really buying these items for herself, and was only lending them to her daughter, although she really knew that this was not true.

Having obtained the material she needed for the curtains and blinds from Emersons the drapers, and the Qualcast mower from the ironmongers on the opposite side of the road, she arranged for them to be delivered the following day. Then, catching the tram to Ilford to get those items that she had not been able to obtain locally, she found the Harrison and Gibson department store and obtained the remaining items on her list. Having arranged for these to be delivered the following day, she then caught the tram back to Chadwell Heath, this time alighting at Grove Road and walking along the High Road for a short distance before turning into Reynolds Avenue, and approaching her daughter's house from the bottom of the road instead of the top as she had done before. She was also rather pleased with herself because she had saved herself a halfpenny on the tram fare.

When Mary-Ann arrived home at the end of a very busy day she was grateful that her mother had prepared and cooked their evening meal, and that all she had to do was eat it. When the housework had been done and the pots and pans put away after they had been washed up, the two women sat talking, and Mary-Ann asked her mother what she had being doing all day. Her mother's reply, "Oh, I've just been looking around the shops," left Mary-Ann unprepared for the surprise she was to receive the next day.

The following day was a somewhat easier one for Mary-Ann. Dr McAndrew decided that he would do all the house calls that day, because the pony needed the exercise, leaving his partner to do both the morning and evening surgeries. When Mary-Ann came home late that evening she was surprised to find that her mother had not prepared the meal as she thought she might have done. Surprise turned to concern when she could not hear a sound in the house, and she was starting to get alarmed as she went from room to room, searching for her mother. Her relief when she opened the door to the small bedroom and found her in there was short-lived, when she discovered that her mother had been stitching curtains by hand for most of the day.

Mary-Ann prepared the evening meal while her mother was trying to finish another pair of curtains before it got dark. As she was preparing the meal she suddenly realised that, when she was searching for her mother, something about the house appeared to be different, although at the time she could not recall what it was. When the meal was in the oven and cooking, Mary-Ann decided to take her coat upstairs and hang it up in her wardrobe, because when she had arrived home, she had flung it over the back of the chair in her anxiety to find her mother. Her surprise over the curtains was nothing compared to the shock she got when she opened her bedroom door.

All her second hand bargains had disappeared, and in their place was a brand new bed with a headboard, a wardrobe, dressing table and a chest of drawers. Rooted to the spot in shock she shouted to her mother in the nearby bedroom, "Mother, what has happened to all my bedroom furniture?"

Without looking up from her stitching her mother replied, "Oh sorry dear, I forgot to mention, the nice man that delivered the new furniture, moved all the other items into the second bedroom." Relieved that it had not been thrown out, Mary-Ann asked her mother why she had done it. Expecting her mother to say that it was just a small gift, or something similar, she was surprised when her mother replied, "I was concerned about you sleeping on the settee while I am here, especially when you are working so hard. I realised that I should have given you more time to settle in before coming down to see you, so I thought I would make amends by helping you to set up your nice new home."

Mary-Ann was unable to think of any suitable reply because her attention was drawn to the smells coming from the kitchen, indicating that their meal was ready. After they had eaten, and the dishes had been cleared Mary-Ann decided that it was her turn to undertake a tour of inspection of the house, this time with her mother by her side. She found that all the furniture she had acquired had fitted into the second bedroom, and the third bedroom which was really little more than a box room, had been turned into a study. All her books, which until now had been stacked in heaps on the floor, had been placed in a new book case, and her mother had also obtained a chair to enable her daughter to work at the new bureau she had also purchased. Overwhelmed by her mother's kindness, all Mary-Ann could do was to take her in her arms and hug her.

Before Mary-Ann left for work the following morning, she realised that she was talking to her mother in the same way that her mother had spoken to her on many occasions in the past when she found herself saying, "Whilst I am very grateful for all that you have done for me mother, you must not spend any more money on me. I am earning good money now, mum, probably more than you, and it is about time that you started spoiling yourself, rather than spending money on William and me." After Mary-Ann had left the house Mary continued with her sewing. She realised that her little girl was now an adult, and whether Mary liked it or not, was more than capable of looking after herself in the big city.

On the Friday evening before her mother was due to return to Somerset, Mary-Ann decided to give her mother a small treat, as a way of saying thank you for all that she had done for her during the past week. Having told her mother not to prepare a meal, when Mary-Ann arrived home from work she collected her mother, and they both dashed down the road to the Gaumont cinema to see 'The Thirty Nine Steps' starring Robert Donat. Sitting in the very best seats in the circle costing one shilling and ninepence each (9p) Mary-Ann was somewhat perplexed after the performance, when her mother informed her that the highlight of her evening had been when the illuminated cinema organ rose out of the orchestra pit with the organist playing. The organ continuously changed colour the whole time that it was being played, until it eventually disappeared back into the orchestra pit at the end of the interval. "That doesn't happen in the cinemas in Taunton," was all she would keep saying.

After the credits had rolled, they stood as the National Anthem was played, and then Mary-Ann took her mother to Sutton's Fish and Chip shop, so that she could sample the traditional Friday evening dish of the area. Having collected their 'piece of cod and two penn'th' for two (cod at 4 pence, chips 2 pence), total cost one shilling (5p), they left the shop, their portions having been liberally doused in vinegar and salt. Mary-Ann started to unwrap her portion in order to eat them on the way home. She was immediately rebuked by her mother who informed her, "You can't be seen walking along the road eating fish and chips in your position, dear."

Although she had done so on a number of occasions in the past, she knew better than to argue with her mother on a subject like that. So they hurried home, and warmed the contents of the two parcels up in the oven, before eating them off a plate, with a knife and fork, with Mary-Ann still wondering why they always seemed to taste so much better out of the paper.

The following morning Mary-Ann had her first Saturday morning off from work since she had started at the practise, to enable her to take her mother to Paddington station. They set off early because Mary-Ann had hoped that her mother could catch one of the trains travelling to Minehead from Paddington, to avoid changing at Taunton. To her dismay she found that these trains did not stop at Bishops Lydeard, and neither could she alight at Taunton from them. After a tearful farewell on the station platform, Mary-Ann watched the 1.30pm train depart from platform four, before returning home.

The train arrived on time at Taunton, and Mary found the 4.30pm service to Bishops Lydiard standing in its usual place in the bay platform. As departure time approached she felt the familiar bump as the engine backed onto the train, at the same time that a main line train arrived at the next platform. Mary watched as the express engine was uncoupled from that train, and after seeing the engine disappear in the direction of the loco shed, she was surprised to see the engine that had previously been backed onto her train was now being reversed onto the train in the next platform. Soon she heard Ted, a porter that she knew well from her daily use of the station, announcing that the train opposite would be stopping at all stations to Minehead. She undid the leather strap, lowered the window in the door of the compartment, and poked her head out to ask him, "Which train will be leaving next, Ted?" She put her head quickly back in the carriage so that he could not see her laughing when he replied, "I can't rightly say, ma'am; that's what we're trying to sort out now, but I should stay where you are if I were you." At that moment Mary realised that for all the benefits of the town that her daughter enjoyed, there was no way that she would change them, for the ways of Somerset.

Almost immediately there was a bump as another engine backed on to their train, followed shortly afterwards by the slamming of doors, and the shrill note of the Guard's whistle, and they were away. She had hoped that when she arrived at Bishops Lydiard station William might be there to help with her case, which she was beginning to find was very heavy to carry. On arrival at her destination she was not surprised to find that William was missing, but delighted to see that David was there instead to meet her, and was anxious to hear all the latest news about Mary-Ann. Taking the case from her, David asked a continual stream of questions that Mary tried to answer, but as they still had plenty to talk about when they arrived at her house, Mary invited him in for a cup of tea, so they could finish their conversation. Having put the case down in the hallway David followed Mary into the kitchen where she was going to make the tea.

When she opened the kitchen door Mary thought that she was about to die of embarrassment when she saw piled up in the sink all the dirty plates, and pans that William had used during the previous week. David sensing her embarrassment, simply laughed, took off his jacket, hung it over the back of a chair, rolled up his shirt sleeves, and started to do the washing up. Meanwhile all Mary could do was to keep saying to David, "I am so sorry, I am so sorry," to which David's reply was, "Boys do not expect to have to do the washing up as well as the cooking, even when they are twenty-nine!"

When William eventually arrived home later that evening, long after David had departed, Mary started to scold him for not doing the washing up. William, who now towered above his mother, simply bent down, kissed her on the forehead, and said, "Sorry mum, I kept meaning to get round to it but I never quite managed to; nice to have you back home." It was at that moment that Mary realised that her son had also grown up now and that no amount of scolding would alter him in any way.

The steam lorries that AK owned had all been sold, or scrapped, and the only steam driven units he was still operating were the rollers, and threshing machines. The new lorries required much less maintenance than their steam driven counterparts, and many of the older fitters, and steam lorry drivers had either retired, or found work elsewhere.

By now William had gained a reputation as a steady and reliable driver, and whenever there was a special delivery, a delivery that had to be at its destination by a certain time, was fragile, or valuable, AK always insisted that William should undertake that duty. Although the work on building the camp at Doniford had long since been completed, the company had obtained a number of similar contracts from the Ministry of War, for the construction of airfields throughout the area.

A problem that affected William was that a few years previously, in 1935, a national driving test had been introduced, and he was one of only two people on the company qualified to drive the steamrollers. This meant that he was working long hours preparing runways on the new airfields, resulting in him spending many days at a time away from home. When he was kicking his heels in a strange place in the evening, he would sometimes be asked to roll the local cricket pitch, or roll a gravel driveway if the engine was still in steam.

The few shillings obtained from these activities, together with all the overtime he was earning, enabled him to obtain a second hand Douglas motor cycle. Once he had obtained his licence to drive the motor bike, whenever he succeeded in getting a weekend, or even a Sunday, off from work, he would drive to various locations throughout the country, even managing to visit his sister in Essex during the August Bank Holiday, much to her surprise, especially as he had not informed her that he was coming.

WAR TIME

Although Mary still enjoyed the work she was doing, she found that her steadily increasing workload caused by the growing number of people employed by the company meant that at times she was unable to give as much time as she would have liked to the many peripheral activities that she considered necessary for the welfare of all the employees. Whenever she found time to ponder on this problem she could not find a solution, and consoled herself with the thought that she would be able to retire in two year's time. Alone at home in the evenings, she spent many hours planning what she would do when that day came.

At other times when she was on her own, in the evenings, Mary found herself worrying about the future of her children. Listening to the increasingly gloomy news bulletins on the wireless, she realised that war was inevitable. She knew that William would be called up, and was convinced that he would be a lorry driver in the Army like his Father and that he would also be killed. She also agonised whether Mary-Ann would be expected to go into the women's forces, and if she did not, would she be expected to stay in London even if it was being bombed?

What Mary failed to appreciate at these moments, was the unfailing ability of the Army to ensure that their recruits were placed in trades they were not qualified for.

The first member of the family to observe the effects of the war was Mary-Ann. As she walked to Church on the morning of Sunday 3rd September 1939, she saw groups of mothers taking their children to the local primary school.

There a number of coaches belonging both to London Transport, and to small local coach companies like Grasshopper coaches, were lined up to take their children, and some of the pregnant women, and mothers with babies in their arms, to the mainline railway stations to catch the evacuation trains.

The vicar interrupted the morning service at eleven o'clock, and switched on the wireless he had brought into church just in time for the congregation to hear Neville Chamberlain declare, "that no such assurance has been received, and therefore this Country is at war with Germany."

After the wireless was switched off the congregation sat in silence for a while, immersed in their own thoughts, before the Vicar brought the service to an end. As Mary-Ann walked back to her house afterwards she saw many of those women who had seen their children off on the coaches, and had no idea where they were going, or when, if ever, they would see them again. They were returning to their homes, some still crying; others had red, swollen eyes from crying, but could cry no more.

William was unaware that war had been declared until he returned home from work in the evening, and found his mother crying in the kitchen. Once he had learnt of her concerns, he attempted to reassure her by being flippant, informing her that he intended to keep as far away from any trouble as possible. He also informed his Mother that Mary-Ann would be all right because she would probably go back to working in a hospital, and that the Germans would not bomb hospitals. Eventually Mary managed to compose herself enough to prepare a meal for her son, although she was unable to eat anything herself. As Mary prepared the meal, like William she found herself not really believing what he had said, but at the same time hoping against hope that perhaps he was right.

Mary soon found herself affected by the war. Before many weeks had passed some of the women working in the factory started to receive telegrams from the War Office, informing them that, "it is with regret that we have to inform you that your husband / son / father / brother is missing over Germany / has been lost at sea and must be presumed to be dead / or had been killed in action." Later, in the period following the evacuation at Dunkirk many more women were to receive similar telegrams. Her own similar experience many years before, enabled Mary to understand their feelings, and to help them in ways that others who had not been through that experience could not do.

Every time one of the women came to see Mary with these problems it brought her own memories flooding back, memories that although over twenty years had passed, she had not forgotten. Another problem Mary encountered after a few months of war was that although virtually all of the shirts being produced in the factory were for the armed forces, the Ministry of Labour did not consider that the company was engaged on essential war work. When the Ministry obtained powers to direct all able-bodied women into industry, they were directed into munitions and aircraft factories, or into the Land Army, but not into shirt factories.

When the time came for Mary to find replacements for the many girls who decided that a life in the WRAC, the WRNS, or the WAAF* was preferable to working in a factory, her choice of replacement employees was limited to school leavers, those that were unfit to work in heavy industry, or the elderly, and the situation was made worse because many of the women had no previous experience of this type of work.

Because William was employed on essential war work, laying runways on airfields, he was not called up into the Army until February 1940. After he had completed his basic training of square bashing, he went before the selection board. The sergeant looked at him and said, "What's your trade, son?" to which William replied, "Fitter, sergeant."

"What sort of fitter, son; gas fitter?" was the witty reply, to which William replied, "No sergeant, I was a fitter on steam ... " Before he could complete his sentence, a look of relief crossed the sergeant's face, and he interrupted William to say, "I've got just the job for you son, 'ome from 'ome!" William then found that he had joined the Royal Engineers and was promptly handed a travel warrant and told to report to the Marchwood Military Railway near Southampton, immediately.

As soon as he arrived at his destination, he was ordered by the 'redcap*' in the guardroom to report to a Sergeant Gray in building D10. Eventually he found the building, and the office he was looking for, and promptly informed the sole occupant of the office, who, because he was wearing sergeant's stripes William assumed was Sergeant Gray, that he was reporting for duty. He then received his orders: "Stow your kit in the hut over there, collect two pairs of denim overalls from the stores, and report back to me immediately if not sooner. Remember that all your movements on this camp are to be carried out at the double." William had already learnt not to laugh, or even smile at any unintentional humour by NCOs.

William reported back to the office. Without removing his feet from the desk at which he was sitting Sgt Gray handed William a pad of forms and informed him, "You are to start to carry out a full service inspection on that lot down there," he said, pointing through the gloom to the far end of the shed. He went on, "Notify me on the appropriate form of any rectification work that needs to be carried out." William had already realised that 'that lot' at the other end of the building looked suspiciously like railway engines, and he thought that now was probably the best time to explain to the sergeant that he had never worked on a railway engine in his life.

As William attempted to explain, a look of total disbelief came across the sergeant's face and, taking his feet off the desk, he picked up a sheaf of papers off the desk, glanced through them, and said to William, "But it says here that you have worked on steam engines." "Yes," replied William. "On steam traction engines and lorries: not railway engines." Flinging the papers back on the desk the Sergeant said, "Well, you're better qualified than most we get here: that lad," he said, pointing to a man about twenty five years old who was in the inspection pit underneath one locomotive, "his only experience as a fitter, was working on the assembly line at the Morris Car works in Cowley until three months ago."

As William walked towards the end of the workshop he gasped in astonishment as he approached the first engine, when he realised that it was the same type of loco that had frequently passed his grandfather's signal box more than twenty years earlier. "Bloody hell!" he exclaimed. "It's a Dean goods." On hearing his remark the sergeant stopped in his tracks, turned and looked at William for a long time and then said, "If you're not qualified son, how the hell do you know that?"

After William had explained how he had acquired this knowledge, the sergeant became more informative.

"I used to work in the Eastleigh works of the Southern Railway, and although it was a reserved occupation, I managed to join the forces because I wanted to do something different." Later, in one of the numerous NAAFI breaks they shared, the sergeant said to William, "It's a shame you haven't learned more about proper railway engines." This view William was later to learn was not shared by the Captain in charge of the unit, who had spent a number of years in the Swindon works of the Great Western Railway.

They then walked on to the next loco which was in light steam. "What's wrong with that?" William was asked. Fearing that it was a trick question, William walked slowly round the engine, and after climbing on the footplate and opening the firebox doors to check the fire, completed all the paperwork, and then informed his mentor that the sandboxes were empty, the firebars were covered in clinker, that a cork was missing from one oiling point, and that a gland needed packing. "Do you think that you can do that work then?" the sergeant asked, and when William replied, "Yes, Sergeant," he was then told, "Right, get on with it then, son."

After the work had been completed under the watchful eye of Sergeant Gray and had been inspected by him, William was told to climb onto the footplate again for a lesson on the disposal of locomotives. After he had familiarised himself with the controls, he was instructed to drive the engine slowly to the water tower and after he had filled the tank, he was then to take it onto the coal dock. After he had coaled it up, he was to drive it on to the disposal pit and drop the fire, clean out the fire, and smoke box, and when the fire box was cool enough he was to replace the brick arch. After he had issued his orders Sergeant Gray turned on his heels and marched back to his office.

By the time he had completed all his tasks, William was beginning to appreciate that many of the skills he had learned years ago on the steam lorries and traction engines, would come in very useful during his Army service. He had completed his work and was shining the copper pipes on the footplate when the sergeant returned, and after he had inspected William's handiwork and signed off the sheets he turned to William and said, "Well done, son, we'll make a railwayman of you yet." William was later to learn that it was very rarely that the Sergeant handed out compliments; everyone was more used to him handing out rollickings.

The Dean goods engines which were then almost fifty years old had been requisitioned by the army from the GWR and had been modified at their Swindon Works with compressors added for air brakes, and then painted a sort of sandy colour which William assumed was supposed to be khaki. They were then sent to Marchwood to be prepared for shipment to France to assist the British Expeditionary Force. It was intended that William would be sent with the locos to help to maintain them. However, the debacle at Dunkirk put paid to these plans, and instead they were sent out to Egypt later, but William's services were retained at Marchwood.

Many of the children, and women with young babies had been evacuated from London. A steadily increasing number of able-bodied men between the ages of eighteen and thirty were being called up, except for those on essential war work like railwaymen, etc, and many of the younger women were leaving the area to join the forces, the Land Army or to go into munitions factories. Therefore the Partners in the Mary-Ann's practice thought they would have a quiet time, and it was during this period Dr McAndrew started to consider that this might be an opportune moment for him to retire.

During this period of the war Mary-Ann was called out many times in the evenings by the Wardens in the nearby ARP post, to attend minor accidents sustained by members of the public because of the blackout. Among the injuries she treated were numerous cuts caused by people walking into lamp posts, or other obstructions, tripping over curbs, or cycling into holes that had been left in the roadway by the local council, who, because of the blackout, were unable to put any warning lights around the obstruction, or the hole. Because ambulances were often unavailable to take the casualties to the over-worked local hospitals she found herself setting broken limbs and putting them into splints or plaster casts.

Before long she found herself in the warden's post most nights, sometimes until the early hours of the morning. She would then return home to try to get two, or possibly three hours sleep before starting work the following morning.

Early in 1940 sufficient numbers of the local children evacuated at the start of the war had returned with their mothers after they visited them at Christmas, to enable the local schools to re-open. Their parents reasoned that as 'nothing was happening' they would be just as safe at home. After Dunkirk the LDV was formed. These were the Local Defence Volunteers, otherwise known as Look, Duck and Vanish, later to become the Home Guard, and even later to be known as Dad's Army. At the start they were armed only with pitchforks, and knives attached to broomsticks, and they succeeded in injuring many of the local inhabitants they were supposed to be defending, as well as their comrades in arms.

Many of those involved in the LDV were between fifty and sixty years of age, and some were even older. Often they injured themselves when attending drill parades, or attempting tasks they had not undertaken for the last twenty-five years. Others finished up with hernias, heart attacks, or pneumonia from standing guard at the local electricity sub station, or the local railway bridges throughout a cold Winter's night.

The full horror of war was brought home to Mary-Ann one Saturday afternoon in August 1940. She had walked down the lane to collect her weekly rations, from the Co-op shop in the High Street that she was registered with. This consisted at that time of four ounces of bacon, four ounces of butter, eight ounces of sugar, two ounces of tea, one ounce of cheese, and one shilling and tuppence worth (6p) of fresh meat. It was a warm, sunny afternoon, without a cloud in the sky, and as she waited for a trolley bus to pass before crossing the road, she became aware of the noise of a large number of aircraft flying in formation, following the course of the River Thames towards the East End.

The Air Raid sirens had not sounded, the anti aircraft guns were not firing, nor were any RAF fighter planes from the nearby airfields attempting to intercept them. At first Mary-Ann thought, like many other people standing nearby, that they were British planes. Suddenly a man in the crowd shouted, "They're German planes!" but even then there was no sign of panic. People simply stared at the planes in disbelief, as they continued on their way unopposed. It was only when the aircraft were out of sight that the nearby Air Raid siren at the Police station sounded, and the anti aircraft guns started to fire.

When dusk fell everyone could see the glow from the numerous fires that were still burning in the London Docks. The sirens sounded once again, and more bombers could be heard flying overhead in the dark, on their way to drop more bombs on the fiercely burning docks. Occasionally an aircraft would be caught in the searchlights probing the night sky and the anti aircraft guns would open up. While the second wave of attacks was taking place the local Auxiliary Fire Service was called out from their make shift fire station in a block of recently completed shops that had not been let, to assist their colleagues in the East End. Like the ARP, the Wardens and the Civil Defence organisations, these firemen were all volunteers who had other jobs during the day. Unlike the full time firemen they did not have the most modern appliances: in some cases it was simply a Ford lorry towing a trailer containing a pump and a length of hose, and some ladders, or if they were lucky a primitive version of what is now known as a Green Goddess fire engine.

That night Mary-Ann treated her first casualties caused by enemy action, after the local Civil Defence and ARP workers had dug several people out of the wreckage of their homes. Three houses had been destroyed by a bomb from a damaged aircraft that was trying to return to Germany, and had been hit by gunfire before reaching its target. All that Mary-Ann could do was to give the badly injured casualties a morphine injection and make them comfortable as they waited for the ambulances to arrive.

When they eventually came, she was surprised to find that they were not manned by the local crews she had been expecting, but by crews who had been drafted into the area from as far afield as Hornchurch, Thurrock, and even Billericay. Because they did not know the area Mary-Ann had to accompany them to the local hospital. On the way she realised that many of the men fighting the numerous fires in the area, had also been brought in from the surrounding districts to replace the local firemen who had been sent to the docks.

The ambulance crew impatiently waited to get the wounded into the casualty department as soon as possible, both in the interest of the patients, and because they were aware of the need to return to the scenes of devastation they had just left, where many more casualties were waiting to be collected. Mary-Ann started to walk the three miles back to her house, protected only by her tin helmet from the bombs, and falling shrapnel from the exploding anti aircraft shells.

After only two hours sleep Mary-Ann was called out at 6am the following morning to go to a local church hall. When she arrived there she found that the hall was crowded with nearly two hundred women and children, and a few elderly men. All appeared to be suffering from shock, some had minor injuries, many were in their night clothes, others had no shoes, some had a few possessions they had managed to rescue from the remains of their homes, and all of them were covered in plaster dust. These were only a few of the victims of that night's bombing.

Mary-Ann tried to treat their injuries while waiting for further medical supplies to arrive. Arrangements were made for some of the people to attend the local public slipper baths,* and when they were clean, they were instructed to return to the hall for treatment. By 8am other doctors and nurses in the area had arrived to assist Mary-Ann, but in spite of all their efforts some of the survivors had to be sent to the local hospitals. While the doctors and nurses were busy, members of the WVS* and the Salvation Army were dispensing cups of tea, and bowls of oatmeal to the survivors. At the same time officials of the local Council were trying to find supplies of clothing for them, and to give people emergency ration books and identity cards, and find alternative accommodation for the homeless.

All the time Mary-Ann had been attending to the homeless during that morning, and later during that same day when she was attending her surgery, and attempting to do her rounds, the air raid sirens continued to sound. Wave after wave of enemy aircraft attempted to destroy the nearby RAF airfields of Fighter Command at Hornchurch, and North Weald. Fairlop airfield was also attacked and this was close to the spot where Mary-Ann and her mother had picnicked and watched the trainee pilots doing circuits and bumps two years previously.

The bombers returned again that night, and day and night raids continued for four weeks, although by the end of the second week the enemy had abandoned their attempts at putting the airfields out of action and were dropping their bombs indiscriminately, often on civilian targets. When the

German Air force found it could no longer afford the heavy losses they were sustaining during the daylight raids, they switched to night time bombing. The Battle of Britain had been won, but Mary-Ann and many thousands of Londoners were about to find out that this was the start of a routine that would continue nightly for nearly two years. The only respite from the nightly raids came when the weather was so bad that the enemy planes could not fly.

The next time Mary-Ann saw the men from the local AFS was the following Thursday when they returned to their base at midday, having been fighting fires continuously since the previous Saturday. Their faces were drawn and black, cheeks sunken, uniforms dirty, torn and covered in ash and their appliances damaged by enemy action. After ensuring that everything was properly stowed away and ready for immediate use, they then went home to try to get some sleep before reporting back for duty at seven o'clock that evening.

Mary was the next member of the family to come face to face with the human misery that war was capable of causing. On 4th November of the same year, 1940, she arrived at Bishops Lydeard station to be informed by a rather solemn-looking porter, "I'm sorry madam, but your train will be a little late this morning; there's been a bit of an accident." When her train eventually arrived some forty-five minutes later, the passengers boarded the train, but the staff made no attempt to get it underway. Instead the footplate crew, the guard, the station staff, and the signalman stood in a rather sombre group by the engine deep in conversation.

Ten minutes later the signalman went up the steps to his box and pulled off the starter signal. The guard walked slowly back down the length of the train, waved his flag, blew his whistle, and the train slowly drew out of the station, only to come to a halt once again before the junction with the main line. After an even longer wait, at last the train started to move forward very slowly, and Mary was completely unprepared for the sight she saw as they approached Norton Fitzwarren station. The first indication of the disaster was the sight of one of the most powerful GWR engines of the King class (No. 6028 King George VI) lying on its side in a field. Then a number of coaches, all of which had been derailed and were badly smashed and lying across the tracks, came into view.

Members of the rescue teams, and many of the sailors who had been passengers on the train, which had left Paddington at 9.50pm the previous evening, were trying to rescue survivors still trapped in the wreckage, while the bodies of those who had been killed lay alongside the track. Later Mary heard that the loss of life could have been much higher if another train that had passed the stricken train moments before it was derailed had arrived on the scene a minute later. Twenty-seven people were killed in the accident including thirteen naval ratings returning to their ships at Plymouth after shore leave. Fifty-six others were seriously injured.

Mary was even more disturbed when she learned the reason for the accident. The driver of the train that crashed, who lived in London, had found when he came off duty the previous morning that his house had been bombed, and he had spent the whole of that day trying to find alternative accommodation for his family. He had then reported for duty that evening, without having managed to get any sleep during the day. It was then that Mary realised that her daughter had not really given her any indication of what conditions were like in London. Afterwards Mary lay in her bed listening to the enemy bombers flying overhead on their way to Bristol or Cardiff.

With the strict censorship that applied at the time, Mary, like many other people who lived in the countryside and who had experienced little or no bombing, were unaware of the conditions that others in the cities were enduring. Mary was deeply disturbed by the sights she had seen that day, but in the words of the saying at that time, she like many others, 'had to carry on regardless.' This did not stop her from wishing that her daughter would return home, at least until the blitz ended, but she knew that this was too much to ask of her.

ANGLO-AMERICAN RELATIONSHIPS

When they were informed that no more Dean goods Locomotives were available, the thoughts of those in the War Department turned to finding an alternative loco to meet their needs. Initially they decided that the 8F loco that Stanier had designed for the LMS was the answer, but the LMS was as pressed for heavy freight locomotives as the other three main line railway companies, and once again the answer was 'no'. To overcome the problem, Mr RA Riddles, who had been seconded from that railway to become Directorate of Transport Materials at the Ministry of Supply placed an order for two hundred and forty of these locos to be built.

Because Crewe works simply could not build all the engines that were needed in the time available, the work was sub-contracted out to the workshops of the other mainline railway companies, including the GWR works at Swindon. When rumours started to circulate around the camp that many of these engines were to be sent to Turkey, all the personnel thought that they were about to be posted overseas. Later it was decided to send the engines to Turkey in kit form, and two LMS fitters from Crewe were sent to supervise the assembly of the locos by Turkish workers.

In the meantime, William, like all the others at the base, was involved in the heavy overhaul and maintenance of the many small 0-4-0 and 0-6-0 industrial saddle tank locomotives, built by a number of independent loco manufacturers like Bagnall, and Hunslet, which had been bought in large numbers by the War Department, for use in docks and other military installations. These units did not have the facilities to undertake major overhauls and when one was due the locos were returned to either Marchwood or Longmoor for attention.

It had already been decided that the 8F locomotives were too expensive to produce for wartime use, and Mr Riddles had been instructed to design two types of locomotives that were to become known as austerity locomotives. Similar in appearance, one class was built as a 2-8-0, and the other as a 2-10-0. They were designed as a cheap, but rugged, all-purpose go-anywhere freight locomotive with a light axle loading, designed to run on poor grade coal, and to operate with the minimum of maintenance for at least two years.

The first of these engines started to arrive at Marchwood in 1943 to be placed in storage until the Allies opened the second front when they would be needed in Europe. Shortly afterwards a Lieutenant, a recently promoted Sergeant William Hawkes, and seven other ranks were detailed to proceed to Cardiff, to assist with the unloading of essential supplies in the docks.

Somewhat unhappy with their new assignment, but knowing better than to complain, they climbed aboard a 15 cwt truck that was to take them and their kit bags to Southampton Station. They wondered what sort of reception they would get from the dockers, who, from the stories they had heard, were even more militant, and bloody-minded in war time, than they had been in peacetime. On arrival at the station William was surprised to find waiting to take them on their journey, two clerestory (ventilated) coaches finished in a rather faded chocolate and cream livery, together with a 'Duke' class engine, another type of engine that he recognised from the time spent with his Grandpa in his signal box many years previously.

With all the place names on the stations removed to confuse the enemy in the event in an invasion, neither William nor any of the other members of his party had the slightest idea where they were going. Finally the train arrived at what appeared to be a main line station, which they assumed was where they were expected to change trains. When they checked with the Guard they were informed, "No, Gentlemen, this is Newbury; change at Didcot for Cardiff." Bemused because this was the first time they had been addressed as gentlemen since joining the Army, they remained on the train, and two hours and twenty minutes after leaving Southampton they arrived at Didcot.

After a wait of some thirty minutes, during which time they had obtained a welcome cup of tea from the station buffet, their connection arrived with more modern rolling stock, although it was hauled by a 'Star' class engine, another class of loco that his Grandpa would have recognised.

When they finally arrived at their destination later that evening, they were surprised to be met by an American Army corporal, chewing gum, who strolled up to them with both his hands in his pockets as they got off the train. Without bothering to salute their officer he asked in a strong New York accent, "Are you da Limeys from Marchwood?" After a pause as they translated the question into English they confirmed that they were. They were then told, "Follow me," and when they did so, they found a thirty seat American coach waiting outside on the station forecourt, to take them to their billet. Following the corporal on to the bus, before they had time to sit down the American had finally taken his hands out of his pockets, and had started on a journey that they would later realise was to be the closest they would come to being killed during their entire military service.

On arrival at what had been a commercial hotel near the docks, until it was requisitioned by the War Department, the bus came to a halt with a squeal of brakes. While they were recovering from their ordeal the driver announced, "This is it guys, see ya in da mornin'." Alighting from the bus they reported to the guardhouse, the former reception desk. They were then informed that the cookhouse had closed, reveille would be at 0600 hours the following morning, breakfast at 0645 hours and that transport would be waiting for them outside the front door at 0720 hours. These orders were followed by instructions on where to find their billets. William found that like the Officer in charge he had a hotel room to himself, while the other ranks thought that they were lucky to be sleeping only two to a room.

The following morning the same American corporal, together with his bus, was waiting outside to take them on another death-defying half mile trip to the docks. After this experience their officer decided that his squad had a better chance of survival if they marched to and from the docks each day. Once they had arrived at the dockside the Lieutenant disappeared into a nearby building for instructions. They later found out that it was the American PX unit,* the equivalent of the British forces NAAFI* but much better stocked. They did not see him again until later that evening, a procedure that he was to follow for the entire period they were posted to the docks.

After they had waited around for about thirty minutes, an American officer, in a impeccable uniform and wearing two silver bars on his shoulder, arrived and informed them that he was Grant Thornton and would they please follow him. William started to line up his squad to march behind the American officer, but before he was able to do so, the American looked back at them in puzzlement and when he finally realised what they were trying to do, told them, "Come on you guys; we ain't got time for all that crap."

Following behind him in groups of two or three, they came to a dock where three locomotives unlike any that they had seen before were standing. They soon learnt that these engines had been specially built to the British loading gauge by three of the largest locomotive manufacturers in the United States, Alco, Baldwin, and Lima. As William was to put it later, "With all their plumbing on the outside they looked massive compared to their British counterparts."

It was at this moment that Anglo American relations took a nose-dive, when Grant Thornton turned towards them, at the same time pointing to the three new arrivals on the dock, and announced, "At last you guys have got some real engines to use, instead of those toys you've had up to now." William only just managed to stop himself replying, "Toys they might be, but at least they hold the world speed record for steam locos!" He had no idea what rank the American held, but assumed that two silver bars out-ranked a Sergeant, and as he wished to retain his recently acquired stripes a little longer, not simply because of the extra money, he decided to keep his mouth shut.

They were then informed that these locos were the new 2-8-0 locos built for the USATC* known as the type S160. The locos had been designed and built for use by the allied forces after they had invaded Europe. They soon learned that it would be their task to check the locos as they were unloaded from the ships, and ensure that they were not damaged. They were then to lubricate them, and after the full acceptance check was completed they were to be put in mid gear, and the brakes released, so that they could be hauled to the Swindon works of the GWR. There vacuum brakes would be fitted, the ashpans modified to meet the current blackout regulations, the tyres re-profiled, and handbrakes fitted to the tenders.

Later, when Swindon works were unable to handle all the engines allocated to the GWR on a temporary basis, some engines were sent to Newport Ebbw Junction for this work to be carried out. Before D Day arrived a total of 174 of these engines were working on the GWR. The allocation of these engines to the GWR, and the other British main line companies, did not mark the end of William's work at Cardiff.

Several hundred more of them were unloaded and sent to Newport for storage until they could be shipped overseas.

William was later to learn that Grant was not a regular member of the American forces, but that he had been employed at Baldwins, as a member of the design team working on the S160 locomotives. After the initial production problems had been overcome, he had been seconded to the USATC to supervise the commissioning of the engines in England, and on the continent.

After a few days William, like the other members of his unit, was struck by the informality prevalent in the American forces. Other ranks never seemed to salute their officers, and the officers did not appear to take exception to being addressed by their Christian names by the GIs themselves. During the breaks while they were waiting for ships to berth, or more frequently for the dockers to finish one of their many breaks, William found that it was very easy to converse with Grant on a wide range of subjects.

He soon became aware that whatever subject was being discussed, sooner or later Grant would inform anyone who cared to listen, that in Texas the subject of their discussion would be bigger, faster, better, or cheaper. One example of the sort of thing that could happen occurred when they were discussing the merits of the countryside that they each called 'home'. Grant talked at length about the wide open spaces of Texas, whereas William spoke about the varied scenery that could be found in Somerset, the levels, the Mendips, the Quantocks and Exmoor. Grant, who for once seemed impressed, suddenly exclaimed, "How far away is this Somerset place you're talking about?"

"Well, in a straight line it's only about twenty two miles."

Grant replied, "Hell, perhaps we could borrow a jeep one evening, and have a look!" On being advised that it was impossible to nip over for an evening, Grant replied, "Gee, we travel further than that into town just to pick up the weekly groceries."

Because, like many other Americans, Grant always seemed anxious to impress his hosts, whenever there was an opportunity to even the score, William and his companions never missed their chance. One evening they were waiting for the dockers to return, to enable them to complete the unloading of another ship they were working on, and release it, so that it could sail on the next tide. They watched an American Liberty ship, loaded with Sherman tanks, many hundreds of which had already been unloaded in the next dock, manoeuvring to enter the nearby lock gates. Suddenly, as the ship was about to pass through them, she was caught either by the tide, or a gust of wind and the ship swung to port and collided with the dock gate causing severe damage to it.

They all realised this would prevent any other ships from entering or leaving the dock for several weeks. There was a stunned silence for what seemed like several minutes, as the enormity of the disaster struck them. Then one of the members of William's group suddenly exclaimed, "Perhaps if the Captain of the ship would let us know when he is going to return, we could arrange to move the dock gates as he arrives, to make it easier for him." After the laughter had died down Grant was seen looking at the ship, at the dock, and then at the group, before replying, "Aw, I get it, your British sense of humour right?"

Shortly afterwards they learned that because of bad weather, and the actions of the U boats, no ships were likely to arrive for a few days. William and two of his colleagues put in for, and were given, forty eight hour passes for the weekend. William immediately sent a telegram to his mother informing her when he would be arriving home. His mother promptly informed her daughter of her brother's expected arrival. Mary-

Ann, who had not had a whole weekend off for over a year, and had not seen her brother since the war started, decided that she would like to spend a weekend in Somerset. The nightly bombing raids had ceased, with only the occasional fighter bomber, or 'tip and run' raid as the locals called them. After confirming with Dr McAndrew that he could cover for her, she set off early on the Friday afternoon, hoping to arrive home later that same day.

William realised that the date of his homecoming was close to his Mother's birthday some three weeks beforehand, and that he had forgotten to get her a birthday card. He soon found that birthday cards were in short supply, because, as he was reminded, "There's a war on, you know," as if he needed reminding. In an attempt to make amends he asked Grant if he could buy a pair of nylon stockings for his mother. When Grant handed over the stockings the following day he asked, "Are you going home to Somersetshire this weekend?" When William replied in the affirmative Grant said, "Gee buddy, can I come with you? I've heard so much about the place from you, it sounds really swell!"

William tried to explain that although he was welcome to come home with him, they only had a small place. Grant exclaimed, "That's alright buddy, I was brought up on a small spread of less than a thousand acres myself." A further attempt by William to explain what he meant, brought forth the observation from Grant, "That's alright, if your Ma can't put me up I can book in at a motel." By this time William had not got the faintest idea what his companion was talking about, and decided that it would be easier to simply end the conversation.

Having left camp earlier than expected, they arrived in Taunton station in time to catch the last train of the day to Bishops Lydeard. After alighting from the train they had caught at Bristol, they were strolling along the platform, toward the Bay platform where their other train was waiting. Grant suddenly exclaimed, "Look at that dame with the glorious gamms!" (Translated as, "Look at that lady with the lovely legs.") This observation was followed by a piercing wolf whistle. Following his gaze, William saw that Grant was talking about his sister, who had ignored the unwelcome attention of the lout behind her, and had continued walking along the platform in front of them.

Realising that he had been given yet another opportunity to score one over Grant, William caught up with his sister as she was about to board the train. Opening the door for her he said, "Hello sis', how are you darling?" Quickly recovering from the unexpected shock of meeting her brother on the station platform she hugged, and kissed him, and after boarding the train she asked, "How on earth did you manage to obtain a set of Sergeant's stripes, did someone lose them?"

After a gaffe of the magnitude that Grant had just committed, most people would have decided that it would be more tactful if they were to travel in the next compartment, or better still take the next train back to their base camp. Seemingly oblivious to any embarrassment he had caused, Grant also entered their compartment. Mary-Ann, realising that a stranger had arrived in their compartment for no apparent reason, looked at William to see if he could offer an explanation why the American had decided to travel with them, when virtually the whole of the rest of the train was empty. "It's OK, sis'," he replied. "This is Grant, a friend of mine; he's come to see what some real countryside looks like. As you can see he's an American, and as you have already heard is completely lacking in tact, taste, and good manners, but otherwise he's a nice bloke."

Immediately after they had placed their luggage on the rack, they sat down, William sitting opposite his sister, with Grant beside him. When they were seated, brother and sister started trying to catch up on all their news, because they had not seen each other for nearly five years. As the train started, Grant changed seats, and promptly sat next to Mary-Ann. Brother and sister tried to continue their conversation, but it became increasingly difficult because Grant would keep edging along the seat to get closer to Mary-Ann, who promptly moved a little further away from him, until she was against the side of the carriage.

Fortunately it was at this moment that the train arrived at Bishops Lydeard station, and they all got out. William walked beside his sister along the road, and because the pavement so narrow, Grant had to walk behind them until they reached the Lethbridge Arms. Suddenly William said, "You two go on, I'll catch you up in a moment," before disappearing through the door of the Public Bar. He did manage to catch up with them, just before they reached home.

Mary-Ann and her brother both noticed the look of concern that crossed their mother's face as she opened the door and found a stranger on the door step. After the introductions had been completed William, aware of his mother's plight said, "Don't worry mum, I've booked Grant into the Lethbridge Arms and I've just brought him in for a proper cup of tea; shall I make a pot?" He was promptly informed by his Mother that, "as tea is rationed, I will make it, otherwise there won't be any tea left for the remainder of the week." William was about to resume his conversation with his sister when he realised that Grant had wasted no time in striking up a conversation with her.

After they had drunk their tea, William informed Grant that he would take him down to the Lethbridge Arms, ensure that he was booked in, and then, because they had received a fresh delivery that afternoon, he would buy him a pint of good Somerset cider. It was at this point that William could have tied his friend to the track in front of an S160 and then run the engine over him: for Grant presented TWO pairs of nylons to his sister, saying that, "They are a present for a beautiful lady." William was seething as he walked Grant down to the pub, and for once Grant was quicker on the uptake than usual. "What's up, buddy boy?" he asked, and when William informed him of the reason why he was so upset, he presented William with another pair of nylon stockings for his mother.

It was not long before Grant managed to create yet another crisis in Anglo-American relations, when, having received his pint of cider he complained that it was warm, then having drunk half of it, he paused, and asked what he was drinking. When William tried to explain as quietly as possible what it was, Grant exclaimed in a voice loud enough for everyone in the bar to hear, "You mean to say that this is just apple juice?" During the silence in the bar that followed this remark, the sound of a wasp frantically trying to get out of the room through the closed window could be clearly heard. After a second pint William made his way home, only to learn the following morning that after Grant had drunk another one, he had collapsed in a heap on the floor, and was carried up to his bed, much to the amusement of the locals. The story of the American who thought cider was apple juice, was still doing the rounds in that bar thirty years later.

When William arrived back home he found that his sister had popped down the road and bought fish and chips for the three of them, simply because they were not rationed and by eating them, they did not use any of Mary's meagre rations. Before they started to eat, Mary-Ann turned to her brother and in a scornful voice said, "William, why did you have to bring that awful man home with you, didn't you realise that this was meant to be a family weekend?" His weekend was not made any better when his mother accepted his gift of the nylon stockings and informed him, "I shall keep these for best, dear," which he knew from past experience meant that she would never wear them.

The following morning did nothing to improve William's spirits when he was informed by the two women that, as he had brought his 'guest' to see the countryside, he had better collect him from the Lethbridge Arms, and show him the local sights. He was told that under no circumstance was he to bring him back to the house in the evening, because they had planned to spend a family evening together.

Even the sight of his friend struggling to eat his meagre breakfast and obviously suffering from a massive hangover failed to cheer William up. After they had left the pub William's day continued to go from bad to worse, when no matter what local landmark, or custom William described to him, all Grant would say was, "Yeah, yeah," before trying to turn the conversation back to his sister Mary-Ann. "Is she really a Doctor?" he repeatedly asked William. "Did she hear my remark on the station? Have I offended her? Could I take her out for a meal tonight?" Unable to answer any of the questions honestly, he was glad when it was time to deliver his 'guest' back to the Lethbridge Arms, and return home to the rest of his family, only to be informed as he walked in the door, that it was his turn to get the fish and chips.

As soon as William had gone out of the door that morning, Mary-Ann, concerned at her mothers severe weight loss, had started to question her about her state of health, and tried to persuade her mother to go to the local surgery with her that morning, for a check-up. In spite of Mary-Ann using all her powers of persuasion, her mother continued to insist that she was all right, but like everyone else she always felt hungry, and that she would be glad when all this rationing ended. Further questioning revealed that her mother was worrying about William, David, and Mary-Ann herself, and this, together with the problems she was faced with at work, meant that she was not sleeping very well.

Finally Mary-Ann made her mother promise that she would go to her Doctor for some sleeping tablets on Monday, and that in future she would go to the British Restaurant* near the factory for a warm meal at midday, because as Mary-Ann had correctly surmised, she was not bothering to cook for herself when she came home tired in the evening.

The time to themselves was brought to a premature end the following morning, when, as soon as he had finished his breakfast, settled his bill, and booked out of the Lethbridge Arms, Grant came to the house, to speak to Mary-Ann. As soon as she heard him at the front door Mary-Ann had fled upstairs to her room, and refused to reappear until it was almost time for them to leave to catch their train. William had already been informed by his sister during the previous evening that they would be leaving before midday, to avoid her mother using any of her precious rations to feed them. Mary-Ann had risen early on Sunday morning and prepared a meal for her mother, and before she left, had placed it in the oven for it to start cooking, in order to be certain that her mother ate well that day.

On their way to Taunton, Grant ensured that he walked, and sat, alongside Mary-Ann for the entire journey. Before they parted at Taunton station he asked Mary-Ann if he could have her address, so that he could write to her, and hopefully they could arrange to meet again. She replied, "I really don't think so. I'm extremely busy, and have very little time to write letters even to my friends. I would think it very unlikely that we would ever meet again."

This stinging rebuke did not stop him from asking William for her address later, so that he could write to her because, as he said, he was sure that if they got to know each other better, they could become really good friends. What

Grant did not know was that on the pretence of giving William a hug before they parted at the station, Mary-Ann had whispered in her brother's ear, "If you give him my address I will kill you."

LOSS AND GAIN

Mary had intended to retire when she was sixty years old, but because the company had been unable to find a replacement for her, she had been asked if she would carry on until they obtained a suitable candidate, even if this meant that she would be working until the end of the war, if necessary. Out of loyalty to the firm that had offered her so many opportunities she had reluctantly agreed. She now found her journeys to work much lonelier without the company of David, who had been forced to retire some eighteen months previously on the grounds of ill health.

He had found the walk to and from the station at each end of the journey increasingly difficult to manage, taking him over twenty minutes to cover the half mile distance, which for the last few months before his retirement, he had only been able to manage with the aid of a walking stick. Finally failing eyesight meant that he could no longer read his beloved ledgers, even when he obtained glasses with the thickest lenses.

Every evening on her way home from work Mary would call into David's house and cook him a meal, before returning to her own home, by which time she often felt too tired to cook anything for herself. Her daughter had correctly guessed that this was the problem, and that is why she insisted that her mother went to the British Restaurant each day. Mary had kept David's ration book and she always collected his rations, when she collected her own on a Saturday morning. After putting her own shopping away she would then walk down to David's house to deliver his groceries, and any other items that she knew he needed.

On a Saturday morning in June 1944, some months after the visit of the family, Mary followed the same routine she had followed ever since David had retired, but after repeatedly knocking on his door she failed to get any reply. When she noticed his half-pint of milk was still on the door step she knew something was wrong, and after checking with the neighbours that they had not seen him that morning, she went straight down to the police station to explain what had happened.

After she had described the situation, the constable who had known David for some time, agreed that she was right to be concerned, and he immediately put the sign on the door of the police station, before he locked it, to tell any callers who might need his assistance that he would be back in thirty minutes. Arriving at David's house it was the constable's turn to bang on the knocker, and the door without success. Asking Mary to remain by the front door, the constable then went round the back of the house to see if he could see any sign of life. After what seemed an interminable length of time the front door was opened by the constable, who had made a forced entry at the back of the house. He invited her in, took her into the sitting room and suggested that she sit down. Then he informed her, "I've conducted a search of the house, Mary, and it would appear that David has died in his sleep. I'm sorry, but at least he seems to have gone peacefully."

Mary had prepared herself for this since she had first knocked at the door with no response.

"May I see him, for one last time?" she asked.

"Yes, of course," agreed the constable.

When she came back into the sitting room, he told her that he would make all the necessary arrangements for the body to be taken to the mortuary. Later that same afternoon when Mary had found that she could not cry any more, she was sitting, thinking of all the happy times that she and David had spent together, and of the great kindness he had shown her over the years, when her thoughts were interrupted by someone knocking at the front door.

When she answered it she found the local policeman on the doorstep. After she had invited him in and made them both a cup of tea he brought her up to date.

"As with all cases of sudden death, there will have to be a post mortem, which will be held on Monday. I don't expect that there will be any problems, so that the body could probably be released for burial later on that Monday." He then added, "I have made a number of enquiries both in the village, and in Taunton, and I have not been able to locate any of his near relatives. Do you know of any, Ma'am?"

After carefully thinking about the question for a time Mary replied, "Well, no – the only relatives of his that I've known about were his mother and father, both of whom died many years ago."

As requested Mary gave him the former address of David's parents, so that his colleagues in Taunton could make further enquiries. As he turned to leave, the constable said, "If we can't find any next of kin we will have to arrange for a Parish burial." Shocked to think that her friend for so many years would be buried in this manner, Mary responded, "No, that won't be necessary; if you can't find any relatives, I will make all the necessary arrangements myself, and pay for his funeral."

The following afternoon, having eaten much better than she had done for many months, because she had eaten David's meat ration, as well as her own, she was now feeling rather guilty, even though she was still trying to convince herself that it would have been an even worse crime to let it go to waste. Her thoughts were disturbed by a knock at the front door, and once again she found that it was her friend the constable, who this time refused her offer of a cup of tea, before telling her that they had not found any next of kin.

"So I need to confirm if it would be in order for us to notify the authorities that you will be making all the arrangements, so that we can release the body to you." She agreed that this was an acceptable arrangement.

The following morning, Monday, as soon as she arrived at work, Mary informed the Managing Director of the reason why she would be unable to come into work the following day. He immediately responded, "Indeed, you must take the rest of the week off. And furthermore, I would ask you to let me know when, and where, the funeral will be taking place, so that I can attend."

Once the body had been released by the Coroner, and she had notified the registrar of the death, Mary made arrangements with the Rev. John du Boulay Lance for the service to be held at the Church of St Mary the Virgin in Bishops Lydeard on the following Friday at eleven o'clock.

Mary had already written to both Mary-Ann and William and told them that David had died. As soon as she had finalised all the arrangements with both the vicar and the undertaker, Mary again wrote to both her children to tell them of the arrangements she had made, in the hope that they could attend the service and help her through what she knew was going to be an ordeal for her. She was a little disappointed when her daughter wrote back to tell her that she would be unable to get down for the funeral, but she enclosed a postal order in her letter to cover the cost of a wreath.

It was only much later that Mary learned that the reason why Mary-Ann was unable to attend, was because the Germans had started to launch the V1* bombs at London, and she was busy dealing with the many civilian casualties that were incurred in her area, every day, and during the nights as well. Her letter to William remained unanswered because she had sent it to his billet in South Wales two days after he had been posted to Longmoor, and although her letter was redirected by the Army, it did not catch up with him until after the funeral had taken place

On the morning of the service Mary was surprised to receive a letter from a Taunton solicitor informing her that he had important news that would be of benefit to her, and asking her to contact him and make an appointment to meet him, at the earliest possible moment. Mary placed the letter to one side and thought no more of it.

Mary arrived at the Church very early on that Friday morning, so that she could recall in the beautiful surroundings of the church the many happy memories of the times she had spent with David, the help he had given her over the years, and how different things might have been. As the time for the service to start approached, she began to wonder if she would be the only member of the congregation when, about five minutes before the service was due to start, a number of the villagers who had known David arrived for the service. As Mary sat quietly waiting for the service to begin, she became aware of a slight disturbance at the back of the Church and the tears started to flow again, when she saw that many of her colleagues from the factory who had known David were filing into the church for the service, including Directors, Managers and many of those who had worked in the office with him, and others who had known him.

After the service was over she went into the churchyard for the internment, and was amazed at the large number of floral tributes that were at the graveside. The great spreads of the past at funerals were no longer possible because of the severe food rationing, and all Mary could do was to invite everyone back to the Lethbridge Arms for a quiet drink after the service, but many members of the congregation were unable to accept her invitation because they had to go back to

138

work. Before they did so, Mary was able to thank them all for coming.

Mary returned to work on the following Monday morning, and as she sat trying to catch up on the backlog of work that had accumulated during her absence, the telephone rang. Answering it, she found that it was the solicitor who had written to her, asking if she had received his letter. When she replied that she had, he asked if he could confirm when she would be able to meet him, because it was now a matter of some urgency, and he needed to see her without delay. Because of the pressure of work she tried to avoid making the appointment for as long as she possibly could, but because he was so insistent she finally agreed to meet him at eleven o'clock the following morning.

After she had cleared the most urgent items of post from her desk the next day, and she had apologised to the MD for her absence once again, Mary made her way to the Solicitor's office which was about a half a mile away. On arrival she was shown into his office immediately and when she had sat down he offered her a small sherry, or perhaps a glass of port, both of which Mary declined. He then said, "I suppose you know the reason why I had to ask you to come to my office, and why I had to see you so urgently?"

From the puzzled look on Mary's face the solicitor realised that she had not the faintest idea why he had asked her to come to his office, so he quickly continued, "The reason I had to meet you was so that I could read the last will and testament of the late David James Thompson to you, because you are the main beneficiary." Mary was still unprepared for what was to follow, because she assumed that David, like everyone else that she knew had very little of value to leave to anyone.

The solicitor announced the main clauses of the will. "David has made three bequests; one to Mary-Ann, another to William Hawkes, each of £500. He has left the remainder of his estate to you, Mary, which amounts to £4250, after death duties had been paid." She was surprised to learn that the estate included the house that he had lived in for she had always assumed that, like everyone else she knew, he was a tenant. The Solicitor went on to inform her, "I see from the notes here that when David drew up his will some years ago, and was asked the reasons for the bequests, he had said that he wanted to leave the money to the family that he had always wished had been his own, in gratitude for the kindness they had shown him over the years." As she was told this, Mary was trying hard to keep back the tears. The solicitor went on to tell her, "So it appears that you are now a wealthy woman." Looking up from his papers he saw that she could no longer control her emotions.

Returning to the office, she found that she was unable to concentrate on her work, and for the first time since those difficult days when she had worked with Mr Leader, she was glad when the time came for her to go home that evening. Although she sat at home thinking about her problems for some time, she was unable find a solution to them. Eventually she decided to write to her daughter, telling her what had happened earlier that day, and at the same time asking her advice on what she thought she should do.

A few days later a letter arrived from Mary-Ann (in a scorched envelope, with an apology from the Post Office for the delay in delivering the letter, due to enemy action!) informing her mother that because she could not come down to Somerset, would Mary like to come up to see her on the following weekend? After receiving a letter informing her that her mother would be arriving in London on the following Friday night, Mary-Ann made arrangements to be at Paddington to meet the train that her mother would catch after she left work that evening.

Because the trains were so crowded Mary found that she was unable to discuss her problems until they had arrived at her daughter's house. After a quick meal of fish and chips, they both sat up until very late that night discussing her mother's affairs. Finally it was decided that they would not be able to finalise matters that night, and they should both go to bed.

Although Mary-Ann slept soundly through her first uninterrupted night slumbers (without being called out to an emergency) in four weeks, her mother's sleep was constantly interrupted by the wail of the air raid sirens, the noise of the V1s passing overhead, and the explosions when they came down. They ate their breakfast together the following morning, before Mary-Ann dashed out to take surgery, and later to visit the local Church hall to tend those that had been injured and made homeless that night.

Mary asked her daughter, "How can you sleep through all those explosions, and the noise the bombs are making as they pass overhead?" Mary-Ann's reply, "Don't worry, mum, it's the ones you can't hear that you have to worry about," (meaning that if the engine had cut out then it was on its way down to earth) did little to soothe her mother's frayed nerves. Later, when the doodlebug's sites in France were captured, the V2* rockets rained down on the capital. They arrived without warning and there was no defence against them. This bombardment continued until the launching sites in Germany were captured.

After breakfast, during the short period after the 'all clear' had sounded, Mary managed to get some much needed sleep, until half past twelve when Mary-Ann collected her mother, and they went to the nearby British Restaurant for their midday meal. In the afternoon they discussed Mary's problems again, and it soon became apparent to Mary-Ann that her mother could not make up her mind what to do with David's house: should she sell it; move into it; rent it out to a tenant, or continue to live in, and pay rent on, the small terraced cottage she had lived in for so many years?

Mary-Ann finally convinced her Mother that it would make far more sense if she gave up the tenancy of the cottage, moved all her belongings into the house David had left her, and sold any items that she no longer needed. Mary's next concern was what she should do with the money she had received. It was then that Mary-Ann discovered that her mother had transferred the previous legacy from Mrs Smith into a current account she had opened at her local bank, and that it had not earned any interest in the meantime. It was at this point her daughter suggested that she retained just enough for her immediate needs in the current account, and put the remainder into National Savings certificates, pointing out that each 15/- (75p) certificate that she purchased now, would be worth £1.0.6d (£1.02p) in seven year's time, which is what she intended to do with her own windfall.

After their discussion Mary was asked by her daughter if she would like to go for a short walk before it got dark. As they walked round the neighbourhood, her daughter found herself wondering how her mother managed to solve other people's problems so easily, and yet seemed unable to resolve her own. It was at that moment that Mary-Ann realised that since she had obtained her degree, she had not had any monetary worries, and indeed she had accumulated quite a nice sum in her bank account. Her mother, however, had never had any money to spare, largely because of the sacrifices she had made to ensure that her daughter had received a good education, and that both she and her brother had not gone without anything they needed. So it was that at this moment her mother was faced with a problem that she had never encountered in her life before.

At this point Mary-Ann felt very humble, and at the same time grateful for all that her mother had done for her. Meanwhile her mother, unaware of what was going through her daughter's mind at that moment, was immersed in her own thoughts, as she noticed the changes that had taken place in the area since her previous visit. In every road including the one that Mary-Ann lived in, there were piles of rubble where houses had been demolished by enemy bombs, and many other houses showed signs of blast damage, with many broken windows some of which had simply been boarded up, because there was no glass available. Similarly, some damaged roofs had been repaired, whereas others still had tarpaulins stretched across their roofs as they waited to be repaired.

Mary smiled to herself as the park-keeper patiently waited for them to leave the park, so that he could lock the gates at dusk, even though the railings surrounding the park had been removed long ago to help with the war effort. Upon their return home Mary-Ann toasted some bread in front of the fire with the aid of the toasting fork, and then spread some beef dripping on the toast, which they ate, as they drank their last cup of tea, before going to bed for yet another disturbed night's sleep.

Mary-Ann was up early the following morning and after breakfast started to prepare a roast dinner for her mother before she left. When Mary commented upon the size of the piece of pork they were going to eat her daughter laughed. "Well, I've found it is useful to have farmers as patients – this joint represents the interest that has accrued on the late settlement of a farmer's account!"

At one o clock they set out to walk to the station, so that Mary could get back home that same evening. As they stood on the platform waiting for their train to arrive, she noticed that most of the buildings on the other platform had been destroyed in the air raids. The station clock which had obviously been badly damaged in the blast, had a hand-written notice attached to it which simply read, 'me no ticky no more'. As they boarded the train, Mary-Ann informed her mother that they were lucky that any part of the station was still standing. "Earlier in the war, the parachute of a landmine became entangled in that tree at the end of the platform. When daylight came they found that the landmine had been dangling directly over the railway track, and that trainloads of munitions, and aviation fuel had been passing by less than fifteen feet below it all night."

Because it had been dark when she had arrived on Friday night Mary had been unable to see the damage that the East End of London had sustained from the bombing raids. As they approached Ilford station the train was brought to a stand still. After a few minutes it was allowed to pass slowly by an incident, where rescue crews were still trying to recover bodies from the remains of a building alongside the railway line, that had been destroyed by a buzz bomb less than two hours earlier. The sight instantly reminded Mary of the train crash she had seen four years ago, and even Mary-Ann who was used to such sights, exclaimed in a shocked tone, "That was the dairy, and many people used it as an Air Raid Shelter!"

The nearer they got to Liverpool Street station the more severe the damage became, and in some areas it appeared that there was not a single undamaged building to be seen. Mary wondered how her daughter managed to cope with sights like this every day of the year.

The following day, after her return from London, Mary started to make arrangements to move into her new home, and four weeks later, after the last van load of her belongings had left her old house, she sat in it, alone with her thoughts for a long time, before she walked out of the door and locked it for the last time.

ANGLO-FRENCH RELATIONSHIPS

When William learned of the death of David he was devastated. He had looked on David as more than just a friend of his mother's. Indeed, he had hoped that one day David and his mother would get married, so that they could be a complete family again. Because he did not receive the letter from his mother until after the funeral had taken place, he was, as he later informed her, unable to get compassionate leave to attend the service, much to his regret.

As soon as the last of the S160 locomotives had been landed and moved away from the dockside, William's squad had been posted to Longmoor. The last person that William saw as the train pulled out of Cardiff General station was Grant running alongside the train asking William for his sister's address. Remembering what she had threatened to do to him if he did pass on this information, William had to pretend that he could not hear what Grant was saying

On arrival at Longmoor they found that large numbers of the austerity 2-8-0 and 2-10-0 locomotives that had been working on the main lines, had arrived at the camp. With the remainder of the personnel he was expected to ensure that each loco received a heavy overhaul, so that the engines could be shipped to France as soon as a major port that could unload them was liberated, after the opening of the second front.

Some of the first ports to be liberated had sustained heavy damage which had to be repaired before shipments of these locomotives could start, so it was not until October that William and his squad were posted overseas. Because they were required in France at less than twelve hour's notice, they did not obtain any embarkation leave. On the same afternoon they heard that they were to be posted, they were on their way to Southampton docks to board the SS Roebuck, which William noted was a former GWR ferry, and that night they arrived at Le Havre. They slept the night and for the remainder of their stay, in some cattle wagons in nearby railway sidings. After a breakfast of 'iron rations'* and a mug of tea, they were marched back to the dockside and ordered to check over, oil round, coal up, water and get steam up on, thirty six austerity locomotives that were either standing on, or about to be unloaded onto the dockside.

As soon as they had completed the task of commissioning the engines on the 31st October, they were ordered to collect their kitbags, and board the lorries that were standing at the dockgates. They set off across the countryside travelling through the night, and arriving early the next morning at another port that they later learned was Cherbourg. Immediately after they had climbed down from the lorries they were lined up in threes, and promptly marched to their new billets.

Although they were relieved to find that their new accommodation was an improvement on the cattle trucks they had just left, it was nowhere near as good as the hotel that they had stayed in at Cardiff. It was a badly damaged warehouse on the dockside, with gaping shell holes in the roof and walls, and not a single door or window left in the building. Straw palliasses had been stacked at one end of the building on the cobbled floor for them to sleep on. As soon as they had dumped their kitbags they were marched for their breakfast to a nearby field kitchen, housed in a building in a similar condition to their billet.

As soon as they finished their meal they were then marched back to the dockside, and once again they set about the task of preparing locomotives as they were unloaded from the freighters alongside the docks. As soon as the engines were in steam, they were moved away. It seemed to them that no sooner was one consignment of engines cleared from the quayside area, than another ship was berthing with yet more engines to be unloaded, and prepared. They soon found themselves working eighteen hours a day, for weeks on end. Any spare time that they had was spent in scrounging tarpaulins to cover the holes in the roof, and wood, and other materials to cover the windows, to make their billet a little more comfortable.

One factor that made this posting bearable was that the food served up by the field cookhouse was far better than anything else that he had eaten in all the time he had been in the Army. It was only later when they were standing on the quay enjoying a brief respite, while the next ship was docking, that he found out why the food was so different.

An officer strode up to them and after they had saluted him, he informed them that, "I need three volunteers: you; you and you."

William was the third 'you' and he then learned that they had 'volunteered' to assist the catering corps.

On arrival outside the cookhouse they were ordered to climb into the back of a Bedford 30 cwt lorry, and were taken on a tour of the docks, eventually arriving outside the largest warehouse they had seen, which also appeared to be the only building in the entire dock area that was undamaged. They were soon to learn that this was one of the main food distribution depots for the American forces in Northern France.

After they had climbed down from the lorry, and had been shown into the building, they looked around in amazement. Stacked from floor to ceiling in a cold-room were sides of meat, and elsewhere crates of vegetables; more crates of tinned fruit; iron rations which were much better than their own modest fare; boxes containing cartons of cigarettes; crates of Coca Cola, and refrigerators which they were informed contained ice cream.

Before they could recover from the sight of so much food, they were told to load 'that lot' onto the lorry which had been backed through the warehouse doors as soon as they were opened. 'That lot' consisted of sides of pork and beef, vegetables and tinned fruit. When they had finished loading the lorry, they found that there was no room for them to travel back in it, and so William and his two fellow volunteers were told to find their own way back to their quarters.

After the lorry had left, and the three of them were about to set off, they were called back by one of the American sergeants they had been working with. Each of them was handed two cartons (each carton contained 200) of Camel cigarettes which they promptly stuffed down the front of their battle-dress tunics. Although William did not smoke he had already learned that cigarettes were better than currency on the Continent.

As they chatted for a few minutes to their benefactor, they learned that the American forces were also unloading S160 locos in another part of the dockyard, and when William asked if Grant was amongst them the American sergeant said that he did not know but he would find out. After going over to a nearby field telephone, and cranking the handle he was put through to someone who had known Grant and after about five minutes he came back to inform William, "Your Buddy was shipped Stateside about two weeks ago."

At the end of February, after they had unloaded and prepared over two hundred locos, the shipments ceased, and as the Allies had liberated most of France William's Company was split up into small groups and sent to numerous locations where the austerity locos were shedded. William found himself posted to a small town in Eastern France called Epernay. There his companion was a Cockney who had been employed as a fitter on a steam operated beam pumping engine at a water works in London, and like William, he had become adept at servicing railway locomotives in a very short time. They found themselves attached to another group of Royal Engineers who were repairing the railway track, and restoring the railway infrastructure, with the help of local railway workers, in order that essential supplies could travel along the line to assist the allies as they invaded Germany.

It was obvious from the moment that William and Harry, his Cockney assistant, arrived at their new posting that the '*entente cordial*' between the two groups, had ceased to exist long ago. The English made no attempt to hide the fact that they thought that the French were bone idle, with lunch breaks that always lasted two hours or more. They also complained that they were always late to arrive for work, and early departing in the evenings. At the smallest perceived slight, or the first indication that any hard work was needed, the French would down tools, and disappear for the rest of the day, leaving the English to carry on working, because the Frenchmen knew that if the soldiers downed tools they would be court-martialled. As one of them informed William shortly after his arrival, "Your people destroyed the railway, you should rebuild it!" It was obvious that in this part of France at least, the joy of the liberation had been short-lived, and many of the locals preferred to remember Dunkirk.

After he had completed his work detail one afternoon, unable to find anything else that he could usefully do, and anxious to get away from the hostile atmosphere in the workshops, William strolled into the town. It was a hot and dusty day, and as he turned around to walk back to the base, he decided to try a little of the local wine. He took a seat at a table on the pavement outside a small café nearby. A young waitress came up to his table and said, "*Parlez vous Francais?*" As this was about the only French phrase that he knew, William shook his head to indicate that he could not, where upon the girl said in perfect English, "You are English then?   What would you like to drink?"   When William informed her that he wanted to try the local wine, she seemed delighted, because unlike the rest of the soldiers who came to the restaurant, he had not ordered a beer.   She then sat down at the table beside him and started to explain that this part of France was famous for its Champagne, but that was very expensive so she would bring him a carafe of the red wine that most of the locals drank.

While he waited for his drink to arrive, he found himself thinking how attractive was the young lady who had taken his order.   He guessed that she was about eighteen or nineteen years old, with long dark hair, and pale blue eyes, and a very pleasant personality.   His drink arrived quickly, and after he had finished it she returned and asked him if he approved of her choice of wine.   William informed her, "I do – could I have another one?"   Scampering away, she soon returned with another carafe, which this time he drank rather more slowly, as he relaxed and watched the world pass slowly by, along the main road.   When he had finished she once again returned, but this time she apologised.   "I am sorry that I cannot not serve you again this afternoon, but the bar is about to close, and I must be getting home."

On an impulse William asked her, "Could I walk to your home with you?"

She looked surprised, but after a slight hesitation agreed, asking him to wait for a few minutes as she cleared the remainder of the tables.   When she re-appeared they started to walk along the road.

William found it easy to talk with her.   "Thank you for allowing me to walk home with you," he began, and then went on to explain, "I'm touched by your kindness, because until now many of your country men that I have met have been so hostile."

Stopping in her stride she looked at him for a moment, and then said, "Are you working at the Railway works."

"Yes, I am," he replied

"Do not judge all of us by the people that you meet down there. Because they co-operated with the Germans, they were treated very well by the Boche. You have to remember also, that many of their comrades were killed in the Allied bombing attacks on the Railway."

As they strolled slowly back to her home he learned that her name was Nadine, that she was twenty-four years old, that her brother had been taken away by the Germans in July of the previous year, that she did not know whether he was dead or alive. She also told him that her parents had a smallholding on which they kept goats, and made cheese from their milk.

She in turn learned that his name was William, he was thirty-five years old, he came from a village in a place called Somerset in England. His sister was a Doctor, his mother worked in a shirt factory and that his Father had been killed in the first World War, and was buried near Amiens. As it was only a short walk to her house, and they learned such a lot about each other, this was achieved by their spending a long time talking to each other, after they arrived at the entrance to her parents smallholding.

Before they parted William asked,

"May I meet you again?"

"Yes," she said, "yes, I would like that." She went on to inform him, "I work at the café each weekday, and on Saturdays until six o'clock in the evening."

William was quick to explain, I cannot tell what time I will finish work tomorrow, so if I cannot get away, you are not to think that I have changed my mind – I will be back to see you again, as soon as possible."

As she walked indoors to face the inevitable questioning from her mother, about the man she had been talking to at the gate, Nadine found that she was intrigued by the Englishman who she had just met.

Normally when she served the soldiers she spoke in French, and they in turn assumed that she could not speak or understand German (which she could understand although she was not fluent), English or American, and until now she had believed that all soldiers were alike, whatever their nationality,

As a rule they would enter the café, order a beer, and when she served them they would start to make rude remarks about their drink, the French people, or the standard of service they were getting. At the same time many of the soldiers would either try to pinch her bottom, or grope her, but this English soldier had not done any of these things. Instead he had treated her with more courtesy than she had been shown by many of her own countrymen. 'Would she wait for him?' he had asked. 'Of course I will,' she thought, 'I want to know more about this unusual Englishman.'

As William walked back to his billet he thought not only about the kindness she had shown him, but about her remarks concerning the railwaymen he was trying to work with, and at last he began to understand some of the reasons for their attitude. The following day he did not finish fitting replacement piston rings to a loco until long after the café had closed. The next day was a Saturday and he finished work about two o'clock in the afternoon. When he had showered and had pressed his battle-dress trousers and tunic, he went down to the café for something to eat as well as a drink.

On the Friday afternoon Nadine had looked in vain for her Englishman, and although she realised the problems he faced in getting away from his unit, she was still disappointed that he had not managed to meet her, although she continued to hope that he would return. On the Saturday it was very busy in the café that afternoon, and she looked out for him each time the door opened, and she became more despondent when he did not appear. It was only when she turned to serve the soldier at the table in the corner of the café, and she saw him sitting there, that she realised just how much she had been looking forward to seeing, and talking to him again.

When she asked him what he wanted, he said he wanted something to eat, together with a carafe of red wine. After he had studied the menu for some time he asked, "What would you recommend?" Before she could answer he indicated that he wanted to say something quietly to her. When she bent down to hear him, he whispered in her ear, "And not too much garlic please, as I am hoping that I will be able to kiss you later!" As she straightened up she found herself blushing as she replied, "In that case, it will have to be a special dish for you monsieur!"

After a leisurely lunch of soup, with half of a freshly baked French loaf, and a *croque monsieur*, washed down with a carafe of red wine William sat and waited for Nadine to finish work. As they left the café together she put her arm through his, and steered him in the opposite direction to the way they had gone two days earlier. In response to his questioning look, as soon as they were out of earshot of the others who had left the cafe at the same time as them, she whispered, "I thought you wanted to kiss me: well, I'm not going to let you kiss me outside my house, with my mother peering at us from behind the curtain, and all the neighbours looking on."

After crossing the road they entered a small wooded copse, with a footpath running through it. They ignored the first seat alongside the path, which could be seen from the road but when they reached the second seat which was hidden from the road by some bushes, she paused, sat down and pulled him down on to the seat beside her. He hesitated for a moment, and as he sat gazing into her eyes, she put her hand round the back of his head, pulled him towards her, and kissed him in a manner that the girls in England had never kissed him before.

When they eventually parted in order to regain their breath she said, "I must go now otherwise they will be asking why I am late." She then stood, buttoned up, and straightened her coat, while William did up his battle-dress tunic and combed his hair. They then resumed their walk, only for Nadine to get a fit of the giggles after a few paces as she recounted the conversation that she had that afternoon with the chef at the cafe, when she had relayed William's message that he did not want any garlic.

"'Why no garlic?' he kept asking," said Nadine, and her answer, repeated several times that, "I have no idea why the customer does not want garlic!" This had failed to satisfy his curiosity, and it was only when the chef made a move to go over to his table, and ask William why he did not want garlic, that Nadine, concerned that William might tell him the truth, suddenly blurted out, "It's probably because he's English." The chef had then paused for a long moment, stared at Nadine and said, "Ah, English, I see!" and seemed satisfied as if that explained everything.

They were still giggling when they arrived outside her house, and William asked Nadine, "Can I see you again tomorrow, because I have arranged to get the day off."

When she playfully asked, "Do you really want to?" William was about to give her a friendly smack for her cheek, when he saw the front room curtains twitching as her mother sat looking at them, and he decided that perhaps it was best if he did not do so, at least on her doorstep.

The following morning he arrived at her house at ten o'clock as they had arranged, and was met at the door by a very serious looking Nadine who said to him, "I think you had better come in for a moment." After shutting the door behind him, she lead the way along a passageway into a room at the back of the house, and when his eyes became accustomed to the gloom, he saw an elderly lady dressed in black sitting at a scrubbed deal table. As William entered the room Nadine turned and said to him, "William, this is my mother." Turning to her mother Nadine introduced William, and her mother then spoke to Nadine in a low monotone voice. William did not understand what was said, and was surprised at Nadine's reaction, for her voice rose an octave, and a torrent of words followed, which once again William was unable to follow.

When Nadine paused while she attempted to regain her breath, her mother appeared to repeat her original remarks in the same monotonous tone, to which Nadine replied in an even shriller manner, and this pattern of conversation went on for several minutes. Eventually Nadine turned to William with tears brimming in her eyes, and her bottom lip trembling and said, "She does not trust soldiers, and before I can go out with you she wants to see your identity papers." William then thrust his paybook at the old woman which she took, and then laboriously wrote down his name rank and service number. When she handed back his paybook, he attempted to make a joke of it by saying, "Under the Geneva Convention that is all the information I am allowed to give you!" but his attempt at humour failed to raise even the faintest smile.

After he had taken his paybook from her mother, Nadine turned to William and said with anger in her voice, "Now that my Mother has succeeded in humiliating you, I suppose that you will not want to go out with me again?"

William replied, "I have come to see you, not your mother, and of course I still want to take you out." As soon as she heard him say that, Nadine grabbed his hand, and, as they rushed out of the house, she collected a wicker basket covered with a red cloth which contained their picnic.

They walked up the road in silence until they reached a group of people in what for the French passed as a queue waiting for the next bus. When it arrived William saw how few empty seats there were on it, and how many people were waiting to board, and he came to the conclusion that they would have to wait for the next bus whenever that might be. As soon as the bus came to a standstill the crowd started to surge forward as the people boarded the ramshackle vehicle. Suddenly, when they were near to the entrance of the bus a problem occurred. Just in front of them was a large lady dressed in black with a matching black shawl carrying a large tin slipper bath, who managed to get jammed in the doorway of the bus. Suddenly there was a huge push from behind them, the large woman and her bath shot through the doorway of the bus like a cork out of a bottle, together with several more people including William and Nadine who suddenly found themselves on the bus together with everyone else who had been waiting in the queue.

The next problem came when the driver tried to put the bus in gear, and found that he was unable to do so because of the crush of people on board. It was at this point that everyone had to try to ease themselves back far enough for the driver to engage gear, and this performance was repeated every time he needed to change gear. For some reason all the passengers seemed to find the situation extremely funny, and before long everyone, including William, was laughing, even though he had no idea what the joke was. After a while a little man who was only four foot six inches tall appeared underneath William's elbow, waving what appeared to be a book of raffle tickets and repeating a word that William could not hear above the general hubbub. The little man was unshaven, wearing a grubby collarless shirt, trousers that had several tears in them, which, fortunately for the lady passengers, revealed that even on a hot day like that he was wearing army issue long johns. William looked at Nadine for guidance. She tapped the little man on the shoulder and handed him a few centimes, and she was given two bus tickets. It was then time for them to fight their way to the front of the bus to alight.

After they had left the bus they walked along the road for a short distance. They passed through a gate and walked along a footpath on the edge of a field until they reached a small copse. Once they were in the shade of the trees William spread his battle-dress tunic on the ground, and they sat on it in silence for a while, until William remembered the bus journey, the fat lady, the little man, who he had realised was the bus conductor, and he started to smile. When Nadine asked him what he found so funny and he told her, it was not long before she too was laughing, and the tension that had existed between them all morning started to ease.

William then asked Nadine, "What on earth went on when we were at your house this morning?"

He was shocked when Nadine replied, "My mother does not trust you darling. She is convinced that you intend to seduce her only daughter."

Nadine's eyebrows shot up when William replied, "I have every intention of doing so," before adding, "but I intend to marry her first." Still uncertain whether he was being serious, or if this was an example of the English sense of humour she kissed him and then decided that perhaps they should start their picnic.

After they had finished their meal of fresh bread and goat's cheese, washed down with a bottle of the usual red wine, they spent a long time kissing and cuddling, before falling asleep in each others' arms. When they awoke the sun was going down, and after they had tidied themselves up and collected all their belongings, they hurried back to the main road, because Nadine was convinced that if she was more than two minutes late arriving home, her mother would be walking down to the bar to telephone William's C.O. to inform him that one of his soldiers had had his wicked way with her daughter.

As they waited for the bus to arrive, an American sergeant in a jeep pulled up and said, "You guys going into town?" After they confirmed that they were, he said, "Hop in!" With Nadine sitting in the front seat trying hard to stop her skirt from blowing up round her waist, because of the breeze that came in from the side of the Jeep, and William holding on for grim death on the back seat, it seemed that it was no time at all before Nadine was shouting to the driver to stop before they passed her house. Bringing the jeep to a stop in a cloud of dust, Nadine alighted, but before William could do so the jeep was driven off, with him still in it, and William was deposited outside his billet a few minutes later. What Nadine's mother made of her arrival home in a American jeep with two soldiers William was never able to find out, even though they continued to meet each other regularly after that eventful Sunday.

Towards the end of April, Nadine left the café one evening, feeling rather dejected because her Englishman was not there to meet her as he had promised. As she started to walk home she heard someone shouting, and when she turned around to see what was happening, she saw it was William running towards her in his overalls instead of his usual battle-dress. She stopped and waited for him, and when he caught up with her, he was so out of breath that it was some time before he could recover sufficiently to apologise for being late.

"And I won't be able to walk home with you tonight, because I have just been notified that I am to be posted to a town called Breda. I'm told it is in Holland: I have to get back to my billet to pack my kit bag right away, because I'm due to leave tonight."

Nadine was convinced that in spite of William's assurances that he would write to her every day, she was never going to see him again, and she started to cry bitterly. William could do nothing to stem her tears, because he had to rush back to his billet immediately, and start packing because the lorry was due to collect him and take him to the railway station in an hour's time.

On arrival in Holland William found that he had joined a larger squad of engineers who had been posted to Roosendaal. He soon found out that his new posting was to a large engine shed and workshops belonging to the Nederlandsche Spoorwagon, the Dutch State railways system, situated just outside the town of Breda. They found themselves under canvas when they first arrived, but as the weather was fine that was no hardship. The task of William and his Company was to service the austerity locos that were being used by the Army, but there were a large number of Dutch railwaymen working in the next bay, trying to repair their own badly damaged, or neglected locomotives and rolling stock.

The thing that struck William and the other members of his group immediately, was the difference in attitude between the Dutch workers and the French. Like the French, many Dutch railwaymen had been killed by the allies when their planes attacked trains carrying supplies for the Germans, but they were glad to work with the English, and although they had much less food than the French they were prepared to share what little they had with their liberators.

The Dutch seemed to have a hatred of the Germans that did not seem to be shared by their French colleagues. The British had only been at Roosendaal for a few days when they heard a huge cheer go up nearby, and soon all the Dutch workers were rushing into their bay, slapping the soldiers on the back, and shaking their hands, and excitedly telling them that the war in Europe had finished, and that the Germans had surrendered

PEACE TIME

After Mary heard that the war in Europe had ended, she left her house early the following morning, and on her way to work, went into the Church to sit quietly in one of the pews for a short time, together with many other parishioners who like her, were giving thanks for those members of their families, and friends, who had survived the war, and that they hoped would now be safe. Like many other people who had heard the news the previous day, Mary forgot for a short while, that many others would still lose their lives in the war against Japan.

At their monthly meeting at the end of May, Mary reminded the Managing Director, Mr Granger, who had been appointed some twelve months earlier, that she still wished to retire.

He responded, "Yes, of course, we need to arrange this for you. May I suggest that you give your immediate attention to finding a suitable replacement for yourself: who is better qualified?" He added, "When you have found someone, if you would notify me, then I will interview the applicant myself, without delay. If I agree with your choice, as I'm sure I will, then steps will be taken to ensure that your replacement can start with the least possible delay."

Several weeks went by, and although Mary had seen a number of applicants none of them was satisfactory in her opinion. She was beginning to wonder if she was expecting too high a standard from her successor, when one day she found a letter in her in tray from a Mrs Williams who said that she was thirty nine years old and was a war widow, who had just been notified that her husband had died in a Japanese prisoner of war camp in 1943.

Her letter went on to say that she had two teenage children, a girl of seventeen, and a boy of fifteen. During the war she had been employed as a Civil Servant in the Ministry of Labour, responsible for directing women into essential war work. The letter reminded Mary of the similar situation that she had been in twenty seven years earlier, and she felt that although she would have preferred someone with more experience, this lady appeared to be the most promising applicant to date. She decided that if, after she had conducted the initial interview she still considered her to be suitable, Mary would arrange for Mr Granger to see the lady.

Mary wrote asking her if she could attend an interview on the following Tuesday morning at 11am. When the day came, Mary was informed by the receptionist that her applicant had arrived rather early for her appointment. As soon as she finished the letter she was dictating, Mary asked her secretary to collect Mrs Williams from reception, and bring her up to see her. When she arrived in her office Mary saw that the lady was a blond, as smartly dressed as the limited number of clothing coupons available in those days of austerity allowed, in a navy blue suit with a cream blouse. She wore flat-heeled shoes that were highly polished but well worn, had rather a slim figure, and was carrying an attaché case.

After Mary had read through her CV, she discussed with Mrs Williams the work she had done in the past. Mary then asked her what skills she thought that she could bring to the job: having listened to her ideas Mary realised that although she had some minor reservations about her lack of experience in this work, she thought that at last she had found a suitable candidate. Deciding that there was little chance of getting an experienced Personnel Officer, at least in the immediate future, she considered that she should have the same opportunity that Mary had been given all those years before, because, as she suddenly recalled, she had no previous experience of the work either, when she started.

As soon as she had made up her mind, Mary asked the applicant to wait in her office, while she went along to Mr Granger to discuss the matter. He then agreed to interview her possible replacement in five minutes time. Returning to her office, Mary explained to Mrs Williams what was happening, and then took her along to see the MD. Later in the day Mary was called in to see Mr Granger, and was informed that he agreed with Mary's assessment, and had offered the position to Mrs Williams.

He then went on to say, "I am pleased to inform you that I have just learned that Mrs Williams has accepted my offer, and will be starting her new job at the beginning of August."

Even his request for Mary to stay on until the end of that month, to ensure the smooth hand-over of her responsibilities, failed to diminish her relief, that at last she would be able to retire in six week's time. That night when she got home from work, Mary sat down to write to her daughter to tell her what had happened.

Mary also went on to advise her daughter, that, as soon as she had retired, she wanted to go away for a short holiday, and asked if Mary-Ann would mind if she visited her for a few days. Three days later Mary received a reply from her daughter telling her that although she was welcome to visit her at any time, Mary-Ann considered that she also needed a holiday, and had made arrangements to stay in Bournemouth for the last two weeks in September; would her Mother like to join her for a holiday together? Mary was delighted at her daughter's suggestion, and quickly replied asking if she could make the necessary arrangements. Mary-Ann was thrilled when she found that her mother would be able to stay at the same hotel with her.

On the day that Mary was due to retire, she sat in her office alone with her thoughts, as she packed numerous personal items she had accumulated during the twenty five years she had been with the company, together with the photos of her children; the small clock that she always kept on her desk in case her watch stopped; her fountain pen (a present from David); her own cup and saucer, and a well-used wooden ruler which after careful examination revealed that it was embossed A. B. Leader.

Suddenly her reverie was interrupted when Mrs Williams came into the office and informed Mary that Mr Granger would like to see her downstairs without delay. As she went out of the office, and started to make her way downstairs she wondered what could possibly have gone wrong. She then noticed that the workshop was silent, that none of the machines were working, nor were the operators chattering amongst themselves, which she thought, from past experience, were ominous signs.

When she reached the foot of the stairs she found that all the members of the staff including Mr Granger, all the directors, managers, charge-hands, office staff and operators were standing around in a semi-circle at the foot of the stairs, and as she arrived at the bottom, they broke into a spontaneous round of applause. After tributes to her had been paid by Mr Granger and some of the managers, an elderly lady stepped forward, who Mary did not recognise at first. She soon realised that it was same lady who had retired from the company many years ago, who, when she learned that Mary was leaving the company, and that a presentation was to be made to her, had asked if she could come in to pay her own tribute to Mary, for the kindness that she had shown to her many years before, when she had been knocked down by the milk float. After the tributes were finished Mr Granger presented her with a bouquet of flowers from the directors, and a 'Goblin Teasmade' alarm clock and tea making machine from the remainder of the staff, so that in future she could have her first cup of tea in the morning in bed. Thoroughly embarrassed, all she could do was to quickly thank every one for their kindness, before turning and running back up the stairs to gain the privacy of her office before the tears started to flow. An hour later when she had recovered her composure a little, there was a gentle knock on the door and Mr Granger peered round the half open door and asked, "Are you are feeling a little better now? If so, is it convenient for me to talk to you?" When she said, "Yes," he shut the door firmly behind himself, before telling her, "I wanted to take the opportunity to thank you personally for all the help that you have given me during the short time we have known each other." He then continued chatting to her about the changes that she must have seen, and the many personalities that she had met, since she had joined the company.

His final words as he turned and left her office were, "You cannot struggle home on the train with all those parcels tonight; my car will be waiting outside the main entrance in thirty minute's time, and I will drive you home tonight."

The following day Mary, who had written thousands of letters during the past twenty-six years, wrote the most difficult letter she had ever had to compose in her life, a 'thank you letter' to all the people at the factory.

ALL CHANGE!

When the surrender of the German forces was announced, Mary-Ann, like many others, breathed a sigh of relief, and assumed that at last, after six years of unrelenting pressure, she would be able to relax a little. This dream was to be short-lived: Dr McAndrew had been talking about retiring for some time, and had spoken about returning to Scotland, so that he would be able to go fly fishing whenever he wanted to. Mary-Ann had eventually persuaded him to wait until they found someone to take his place. Although they had advertised regularly in the British Medical Journal they had received very few applications, none of which either of them had considered satisfactory.

At the beginning of August Dr McAndrew announced that he felt that he was unable to carry on any longer in the practise, and that he wished to leave immediately. He informed Mary-Ann that he felt at his age he would be unable cope with the changes that he felt that the new National Health Service would bring. Mary-Ann suddenly realised just how much six years without a break of any kind had taken out of her, and she pleaded with her partner to stay on until the end of the following month, and if he would allow her to take the last two weeks in September off for a complete rest, then even if they had not obtained a replacement, he could retire on the first of October, a request that he reluctantly agreed to.

Finally, when the long-awaited day that marked the start of her holiday arrived, Mary-Ann caught the train to Liverpool Street station, and travelled across London to Waterloo station. From there she caught the train to Bournemouth, which arrived at her destination only fifteen minutes late at 2.16pm. Uncertain of the location of her hotel she caught a taxi from the station, and when she arrived, found that it was on the cliff top, only about a quarter of a mile from the gardens alongside the Winter Pavilion in the centre of the town.

That same morning her mother had caught the train into Taunton, and after a wait of only five minutes boarded the local train from Exeter to Bristol that stopped at all stations. On arrival at Highbridge she alighted, crossed the footbridge to the adjacent station, that everyone called the S&D* station. Walking onto the platform, she found a two coach train waiting, with an engine attached, and learned that it was due to depart in ten minutes. When the departure time arrived, it seemed not to make the slightest difference to any of the staff: the footplate crew sat on the empty four-wheeled parcels truck on the platform drinking tea, the Guard of the train carried on his conversation with the platform staff on the respective merits of their allotments, and the signalman in his box continued cutting the hair of one of his local customers. Some ten minutes after the booked departure time, all the staff decided that perhaps now might be a good time to send the train on its journey.

Mary knew when she arrived at Evercreech Junction that she had to change trains, and that the Bournemouth train was due to depart from the Junction only five minutes after the arrival of her train. When it arrived fifteen minutes late, as soon as she alighted she asked a member of the platform staff if she had missed her connection for Bournemouth, he replied, "No, madam, 'tis Saturday: trains never run on time on Saturdays: it'll be along shortly." Eventually her train arrived some seventy-five minutes later, and she set off on the final leg of her journey to Bournemouth, hoping that Mary-Ann would still be waiting for her when she finally arrived.

Mary-Ann had learned as she was about to leave the hotel to collect her mother that there were two railway stations in Bournemouth, and that her mother would be coming into the

West Station, and not the station at which she had arrived earlier. Because she had no idea where it was located in the town, she was grateful when the hotel arranged for a taxi to call and take her to her destination. Arriving there she paid off the driver and dashed onto the platform, after purchasing her platform ticket, just it time to see a train from Evercreech Junction (the one which Mary had missed by only two minutes) pull into the station.

Her concern mounted as each minute passed, and she searched in vain for her mother amongst the many passengers alighting from the train. It was only when the last person had left the platform, that she learned that this train had arrived over an hour late, and was an earlier one than her mother had intended to catch. Eventually the train she was waiting for arrived, and she spotted her mother amongst the crowds. Mary-Ann took her mother's case and hurried to the taxi rank. But while they waited in the queue for a cab, Mary started to scold her daughter for such extravagance, until Mary-Ann explained that if they did not get to the hotel soon, they would be too late for their evening meal.

That evening after they had finished their meal, they strolled down the hill to the gardens between the Square and the pier, and as the clocks were still set on DBST* it did not start to get dark until well after ten o'clock in the evening. As dusk fell, they sat in the gardens and watched people lighting the night lights housed in small multi-coloured round jars hanging in the trees throughout the gardens. When they had finished there were scores of red, green, blue and white lights twinkling around the grounds. After the years of blackouts, this small gesture was the first sign to many people who saw the display that at last things were starting to return to normal.

The next day they caught a yellow trolley-bus from the Square to County Gate and from there they walked down Alum Chine. They had intended to continue along the esplanade back to the Central Pier, but when they reached the end of the Chine they found their way blocked by masses of barbed wire. For a while they watched Army personnel dismantling scaffolding poles that had been erected at the low tide mark, which it was hoped would have ripped the bottoms out of the invasion barges had the coast been invaded. Other soldiers were lifting mines that had been sown all along the beach to act as another deterrent to any would-be invaders.

After a while they strolled back along Alumhurst Road to catch another trolley-bus back to the centre of town. It was only then that Mary-Ann suddenly realised why these trolley-buses appeared to be so familiar to her. She recalled that at the height of the blitz many of the London trolley-buses in her area had been destroyed or damaged by enemy action, and Bournemouth trolley-buses had been requisitioned to replace them, and keep the local services running.

The remaining days of their holiday were spent catching Royal Blue coaches from the Bus Station near the Square on day excursions to Dorchester or Weymouth. On other days they took a local Hants & Dorset green bus to Poole or Sandbanks, watching or travelling on the chain ferry. Some afternoons they caught one of the numerous small coaches that were lined up in the square, with blackboards alongside each vehicle, inviting people to take day, afternoon, or evening mystery tours of the surrounding countryside. On other occasions they sat in deck chairs in the gardens, enjoying the sunshine and listening to the local silver, or brass bands playing in the bandstand. Evenings were spent in either the Winter Gardens or in the Pier Pavilion watching variety shows, in which acts like Jack Warner, Gert and Daisy, Vera Lynn, and a newcomer called Alma Cogan appeared.

At last their holiday came to an end, and the time came for them to make their respective ways home.

As soon as she returned, Mary-Ann made herself a cup of tea, unpacked her luggage, and then went round to the surgery to let her partner know that she had arrived home. She was rather surprised when he greeted her with a broad smile, invited her into his sitting room, and before she could sit down informed her, "I think I have found a suitable candidate for the practise. I hope that you will approve of, and be able to work with him. I explained that you are the one that must make the decision, because it will be your surgery now. I made an appointment for him to come back next Tuesday afternoon to see you: have I done the right thing, lassy?" he enquired.

The thought crossed Mary-Ann's mind that if he was any good, then perhaps her partner should have taken him on there and then, and locked the door so that he could not escape. Although she was worried that the candidate might change his mind before next Tuesday, she tried to put Dr McAndrew's mind at rest by assuring him that he had indeed done the right thing. When she thought about their discussion later, she realised that apart from assuring her that the candidate was well qualified, Dr. McAndrew had refused to give her any further information about him, saying only that it would be up to her to make a decision when she met him.

The following Tuesday she had set two hours aside, before evening surgery, to interview the prospective newcomer. When she met him, she found that after reading his CV she was very impressed. His name was Harry Marchwood, aged thirty-five, and he was six foot tall with black hair that showed signs of going grey. He had qualified as a Doctor at the start of the war, and had spent five years working in casualty clearing stations behind the front lines in the Middle East and Italy. After he was injured by flying shrapnel in his arm, and legs, when the unit he was working in was shelled by enemy guns, he was later discharged as being unfit for further duties.

After a period of convalescence he decided he wanted what he hoped would be a quieter life, as a GP in civvy street. Married, with two young children, she admired his honesty when he informed her that his previous applications had been turned down simply because of his medical discharge, but he assured her that he was now completely recovered. Having seen the medical report that Dr. McAndrew had prepared after he had examined him, Mary-Ann had no doubt that he was right. After outlining the prospects, and conditions of his employment, she was delighted when he said that he was happy to accept her offer, and that he would inform her, within the next few days, when he would be able to start.

Later that evening after surgery had finished she thanked her colleague for his help, and told him that he had earned his retirement. She also took the opportunity to wish him all the best for his future. Her happiness was shattered when, on the following Tuesday, she received a letter from Doctor Marchwood to say that he very much regretted that he would not be able to start work with her as he had hoped.

Mary-Ann simply could not believe what had happened, because he had seemed so satisfied with the offer she had made. She sat looking at his letter in utter disbelief for almost an hour, and as she did so, Dr McAndrew wandered into the room, and seeing the expression on her face, sensed that something was wrong.

"What's the trouble?"

"Dr Marchwood. He says he won't be coming."

Her partner snatched the letter from her, and after reading it through carefully he said, "Lassie, there's a telephone number at the top of the letter: why don't you ring and ask him to tell you why he has changed his mind?" Cursing herself for not thinking of such a obvious way of hopefully solving her problem, she agreed to do so. Her partner sat on the opposite side of her desk looking at her intently, while she tried to work up the courage to make the call. Finally he said to her, "There's no time like the present, lassie."

The telephone was answered as soon as the operator connected her to the number, and she was relieved to hear that it was Harry who was speaking. Introducing herself, she asked him to give an honest answer to her question, "Why," she asked, "Have you changed your mind about joining the practice?"

He informed her, "Well, to be honest with you, I would still like to join the practice. But because so many houses in the area have been destroyed during the air raids, I've been unable to find any suitable accommodation locally, for my wife and small family at any price." He continued, "After spending so much time apart from my family during the war, I do not want to be parted from them again." After thinking about his answer for a moment Mary-Ann told him, "Thank you for your explanation. I understand your reason for being unable to accept my offer, but if I could obtain suitable accommodation for you and your family, would you still be prepared to join the practice?"

"Well, yes, of course, I'd be delighted to!"

"I will call you back as soon as I have some news," she promised, although as she put the telephone down she still had no idea how she was going to solve the problem. She explained the gist of her conversation to her colleague who was still sitting opposite her, and they both sat in silence for a while. Mary-Ann realised that Harry had told her the truth, and that if she had thought about the matter before, she should have realised that the problem of accommodation was probably the reason they had failed to get anyone to join the practice in the past.

During the six years of the war, over 4,500 of the 4,650 houses in the area had been either destroyed or damaged by enemy action, and although some efforts were now being made to repair the damaged houses, and pre-fab bungalows* were being erected on many of the bomb sites, the shortages of materials and the men available to carry out the work, meant that progress was slow.

Suddenly the silence was shattered as Dr McAndrew brought his fist down on the desk with such force the ink in the inkwell on the desk stand was spilt, as he shouted at the top of his voice, "That's the answer!"

For what seemed an eternity she waited for his solution to the problem, and was beginning to think that he had changed his mind when he continued, "I want to go back to Scotland, but I cannae sell this property because the surgery is attached." Not following his line of thought, Mary-Ann looked at him blankly, before he said, "Don't you see: if you buy or rent this house and surgery from me, I can go to Scotland, you can move in here, and Dr Marchwood can occupy your present house !"

Mary-Ann thought hard about the suggestion for some minutes before saying, "But Mrs Marchwood may not like my house!"

To which her partner, anxious to be retired soon, replied, "Until you invite her to look around it, you are not going to know, are you!"

There followed another long pause before Mary-Ann said, "But the Estate Agents may not be prepared to transfer the lease."

This remark resulted in a snort from the other side of the desk, and the observation, "You leave that with me lassie, I will sort that out, if the situation arises." Another long silence ensued, and then Mary-Ann was asked, "Are there any other problems then?" When she replied that she could not think of any, she was told to telephone Dr Marchwood straight away.

This time when the operator put her through to the number, the telephone rang for some time before Harry answered. Mary Ann explained, "I have found a house that might be suitable for your needs. Could you bring your wife and family along next Saturday afternoon to look over the property?" Harry put his hand over the mouth of the receiver, and she could hear him talking, but was unable to hear what he was saying. She was relieved when he took his hand away from the receiver, and confirmed that he would be at the surgery, at 2.30pm on Saturday, with his family.

After Harry and his family had looked around the house, Mary-Ann realised that he needed to discuss the matter further with his wife, and she informed him that if he wanted to take a another look around the house and the garden before making up his mind, she would wait for him back at the surgery.

When Harry arrived there with his family an hour later, Mary-Ann was thrilled when he told her the good news that they were delighted with the house, and that he would be happy to join her at the practice. Even the bad news that he would not be able to start until the beginning of December, failed to dampen her spirits. Mary-Ann had hoped for personal reasons that he would have been able to start earlier, but on reflection she realised that the later date would give more time for Dr McAndrew to vacate the house and surgery, and for her to move in.

As is usual in life as soon as one problem is resolved another is created. Her little Austin Seven was becoming more temperamental as each month passed, even though Mary-Ann had it serviced regularly, and kept it topped up with petrol, even when her coupons for the month had all been used. Arriving late for a house call one day she apologised to her patient because she had kept him waiting, and explained that her car had expired on the way to see him.

174

"It's about time you pensioned off that old car doctor," was the patient's reply, to which Mary-Ann replied, "Don't you know that all the new cars are going for export, and that it is impossible to obtain one?"

Quick as a flash he replied, "I work at Fords: if you would like me to, I can make special arrangements for you to obtain a new car." Without thinking, she murmured, "That would be nice," as she took his blood pressure. After writing out his prescription, she then thought no more about their conversation.

Three weeks later she was surprised to see her now fit patient appear in the surgery, to inform her that, "There is a brand new Ford Prefect waiting in the showroom of the local Ford dealer with your name on it. If you don't like it, not to worry because the dealer will have no difficulty in selling it, and I will try to get you another type of car!"

After thanking him profusely she went down to the showroom the following day, and after she had taken it for a test drive, decided that it was a great improvement on her present transport, and although her funds were rather low after the purchase of the house and surgery, they would have to be depleted still further because she needed another car. Having sorted out her funds that night, she returned to the showroom the following morning and ordered the car.

Three days later as she drove it home from the showroom, she realised that even as a special deal, the car had cost her almost as much as she had paid for the house. Mary-Ann offered the Austin Seven to Harry, because she thought that as he appeared to be quite knowledgeable about cars, it might be of use to him. She considered she had been honest with him when she had pointed out that the car could be rather temperamental, but it was only afterwards that she realised that she had failed to inform him that the brakes were best described as being inefficient.

Two days after taking over the Austin Seven Harry was following a trolley-bus that had more effective brakes than the car, and ran into the back of it when it stopped suddenly. Harry was uninjured, the bus undamaged, but the damage to the Austin seven proved to be terminal.

It was not long before Mary-Ann found that as with all Ford Prefect cars, you had to take the weather into account when starting it in the mornings. The choke had to be set just right, and the adjustment to be made depended on whether it was raining, dry, hot or cold, and that failure to get the setting just right first time, resulted in the carburettor flooding, and a much delayed start to her day. The other problem that took some getting used to, was that the faster the car went, the slower the windscreen wipers operated, which made life interesting when it rained.

A NEW FAMILY

For William, after peace had been declared in Europe, things carried on for a while in much the same way as they had done for months past. His unit continued to service the austerity locomotives that were being used for military purposes. In October a decision was made to allocate 232 of these engines to the Dutch State Railways, to ease the shortage of their engines caused by allied air strikes, and others that were destroyed by the retreating German forces.

The Dutch railwaymen in the nearby workshops were soon engaged in repainting the engines that had been transferred to them to an olive green colour, with black lining on the cab, and tender sides and allocating NS numbers painted in white on the cab sides. Several other modifications were carried out at the same time, including a twenty-two inch extension to the chimney to cure drifting smoke. A ladder was also fitted to make access to the clack valves easier; the vacuum brakes were changed to air brakes, and in some cases steam heating was fitted.

By December 1945 a large number of the austerity locomotives on the Continent had been placed in storage, whilst others were transferred to the State Railways in Belgium, and France. Some were returned to England, and soon there was insufficient work for William's squad so they were all posted back to Longmoor. From there William was demobilised in January 1946, six years almost to the day after he had joined the Army.

When William had first been posted to Roosendaal he had written to Nadine every day, telling her how much he loved her, and that he would return to Epernay as soon as he could. After the first month, when he had not received a single reply from her, he still continued to write to her every week, but still he did not get any news. By the time he was demobilised he was desperate to find out what had happened to Nadine, and why she had not written to him.

When Nadine did not receive any letters from William after he was posted, at first she blamed the postal system, but she remained convinced that her Englishman would return for her. She was unable to write to him because she did not know where he had been posted, and he had not given her his address in England. By the start of the new year, however, she had decided that she was never likely to see or hear from him again.

Mary was delighted when her son turned up on her door step unharmed after his demob. But her joy was short-lived, when he informed her that as soon as he had raised sufficient money from the sale of his motor bike, which had been in store throughout the war, he wanted to return to France. After much questioning on her part, he told his mother he was going back to France because he had met the girl he wanted to marry. Although Mary could not understand what he found more attractive in a French girl rather than the local girls, she thought it best not to ask. Instead she felt relieved that at long last her son seemed intent on settling down.

Two weeks after he had arrived home William was on his way back to France, after he had written to Nadine to let her know he was coming. Arriving in Epernay just before she was due to leave work William hurried to the café to meet her, arriving outside her workplace as she was leaving. With her head down she walked past him, and did not see him. It was only when she heard a voice that she remembered so well, say in English, "Aren't you glad to see me any more, then?" that she gasped in astonishment, turned and rushed into his arms and kissed, him not caring this time who saw them.

As soon as she recovered from her initial surprise at seeing him, Nadine remembered the hurt she had suffered during the months that had passed since their last meeting. Pushing him away from her to arm's length, she cried, "Why did you not write to me as you promised; couldn't you even let me know that you were going to come back to France?" William was so taken aback at this outburst, that for a moment he could only stare at her open mouthed, before gathering his wits together to tell her that he had written to her regularly. It was then Nadine's turn to be shocked, and after staring at him for some time she decided that he must be telling her the truth. She then said very slowly, and quietly, "But I have not received a single letter from you since the day you left. What can have happened?"

For a long time after William had shrugged his shoulders to indicate that he had no idea, they continued to stand on the corner of the road, silently gazing into each others' eyes. By the time William had summoned up enough courage to ask Nadine if he could walk home with her, a germ of suspicion was starting to form in her mind.

As they walked through the copse, he found himself answering a barrage of questions

"Why have you come back here?" was the first thing she asked.

He replied, "Because I love you, and I have missed you terribly, and I had to find out what had happened to you. I was desperate to see you again."

Before he could say more, she asked, "How long will you be here for?"

Grasping her arm to stop her from walking on, he turned her towards him and said, "Until I can persuade you to marry me, and I can take you back to England with me." She put her arms around him and gave him a long, lingering, passionate kiss. When she finished, and had got her breath back she replied, "I want to marry you desperately, darling, but I cannot leave my mother on her own at this time. My brother has still not returned after the war, and we do not know what has happened to him."

"In that case," said William, "If you will marry me, I will stay here with you, because I cannot bear to be parted from you again."

As soon as they arrived at her gateway, Nadine dashed into the house to tell her mother that her Englishman had returned to see her, and that he had asked her to marry him. Ignoring the look of disapproval on her mother's face Nadine informed her, "I am going out again to find him somewhere to stay for the night, and to discuss our future plans."

After walking round the town for nearly two hours, having been informed by several establishments that they had no rooms available, which Nadine found hard to believe, they eventually found a room for William for one night, in a small rundown commercial hotel near the station. After this room had been booked, they sat for a long time in the bar of the hotel, drinking coffee, while they discussed their future together. Finally William walked Nadine back to her home at around midnight.

The following morning, as they had planned, Nadine asked her mother if she would let them have two rooms in her house until they could find a home of their own. In return Nadine assured her mother that William would help her on the smallholding. Although Nadine had gathered that her mother was not overjoyed at the prospect of her marriage, she was unprepared for her mother's outburst, when in response to Nadine's enquiry she snarled, "I will not allow any foreigner to stay in my home, and I certainly do not want help from one either." She continued, "I have done everything I can to prevent you getting involved with this man, and I shall continue to do all that I can to stop you making this mistake. If you persist in going ahead with this wedding neither you, nor that man will be allowed in this house again."

In spite of her mother's outburst, when they met later that morning Nadine was more determined than ever to marry her William. It was not long before they had made the necessary arrangements to be married at a civil ceremony in three week's time. They also located two rooms to rent in which, not only could they start their married life, but where William could stay until they were married.

The money that William had obtained from the sale of his motorbike, together with his demob pay, had by now all gone, and they were living on the money that Nadine was earning. This arrangement annoyed and upset William very much, and he redoubled his efforts to obtain work. Learning that they needed skilled fitters at the local railway sheds he applied for a job only to be refused. He also applied for work as a lorry driver, as a labourer on a building site, and even helping to pick vegetables on the local farms. But the answer was always the same '*non*'.

On the day of the wedding ceremony Nadine's mother refused to attend, and Mary had been unable to get there because she could not undertake such along journey unaided, while his sister could not arrange for a locum to cover for her, while she was away. Nadine's friends acted as witnesses, and after the ceremony they had a small party in the café where Nadine worked.

William continued to search for work, but he became even more depressed and annoyed when Nadine informed him that some of the people that she had known all her life in the town, and others that she had served regularly in the café in the past, were now shunning her, because she had married a 'Tommy'.

Three months after they were married Nadine informed her husband that she was pregnant, and although William was delighted when he heard the news, he realised that something would have to change, because once Nadine was unable to work any longer, if he had still not obtained a job, their future would be very bleak indeed.

When he first discussed his worries with his wife, Nadine felt that although she had not returned to her mother's house since she was married, she still hoped for a reconciliation with her. For this reason she was reluctant to consider either moving to another location where perhaps William would find it easier to obtain employment, or to move to England, where he knew work was available. Faced with this impasse William told Nadine that the only other solution that he could think of, was for him to return to England alone: obtain work, and then send out money to her each week to support both her and their child. This idea Nadine refused even to contemplate.

While she was still worrying about their future together, Nadine met one of her former neighbours in the street, who told her that she thought that her mother now regretted that she had not attended their wedding. Thinking that at last there was a possibility of the reconciliation that she had longed for, she decided on an impulse to go to her mother's house. Finding the door on the latch, she let herself in and going through to the dining room found her Mother burning un-opened bundles of letters addressed to her, in what she now recognised was William's handwriting, on the envelopes.

Snatching from the table the few remaining letters that had not been burnt, she looked first at the letters in her hand, and then at her mother. She was speechless with rage and the tears started to well up in her eyes, when she realised that the suspicion that she had had in her mind all along, but that she had refused to believe, was true – that her mother had intercepted William's letters.

It was some minutes before Nadine could gain any form of self-control, but when she did, she said in a cold calm voice to her mother, "Why did you do this? How could you possibly do something like this to me?"

Her mother replied, "I told you what I would do, and when that foreigner cannot support you any longer, you will be only too glad to come back to me."

It was only then that Nadine realised that the reason that William had not been able to obtain work was probably due to her mother's interference.

The realisation of what had happened snapped the last bond that existed between mother and daughter. Nadine shouted at her mother, "No matter how hard you try, there is nothing that you can do to part us. We have only stayed in this town because we thought that you might need our help sometime. After what I have just learned, I cannot bear to be in the same country as you any longer. We are going to England, and you will never see us again!"

Without waiting for her mother's reaction, she dashed out of the house for the last time, and her final words proved to be true.

When Nadine arrived at their flat a few minutes later, she was extremely distraught, and although William tried hard to find out who, or what, had upset her it was some time before he managed to stem the flow of tears. She then informed a startled William that if he still wanted to take her to England, she would like to leave as soon as they had packed their few belongings. It was only later that night on the train to Paris, that William found out what had happened, and the reasons for their hurried departure. When Nadine had finished speaking, William sat in silence for a while and then said, "Perhaps this is the new beginning we have been searching ... and hoping for."

Two days later Mary answered a knock at her door, and found one of the managers of the shirt factory on her doorstep. She had known him for many years since they had worked together, and after exchanging pleasantries he asked if he could come in, to talk to her on a matter of some urgency. Seated in her front room, he explained that the company intended to build a new factory on the site of the old wagon works at the far end of the village, to replace the temporary premises they occupied in huts the American forces had built in the grounds of the Sandhill Park Estate. The company was now planning the procedures to be followed when transferring their employees to the new premises. He then went on to explain that they needed another personnel officer, and in spite of all their efforts they had been unable to find a satisfactory applicant: would Mary be prepared to help on a temporary basis until they found a suitable candidate?

To give her time to think about his proposal, she made him a cup of tea, and while he sat drinking it Mary remained deep in thought. She had been away from work for almost two years now, and felt that many of her ideas would probably be considered outdated. Also, upon reflection, she thought that she would be unable to cope with the pressure that she would undoubtedly be expected to face.

When she informed him of her decision, he asked if she knew of anyone else who she thought would be suitably qualified. Eventually, after some deliberation, she gave him the name and address of a friend that she had met at the local branch of the Women's Institute. Mary had learned that the lady had been demobilised from the ATS* having reached the rank of Captain. She also knew that when she was in the forces she had been the adjutant of a large women's training camp, so she thought that not only was she was probably capable of doing the work, but that she might also be interested in the project. After thanking her profusely he rose and she showed him out.

Before Mary had time to worry whether or not she had made the right decision, as soon as he had left she went into the sitting room to collect his tea cup, and then into the kitchen to wash it up. As she did so there was another knock at the door. Assuming that it was her previous visitor who had returned with another query, when she opened the door she was both surprised and delighted to find William standing on the door step, with his arm around a very beautiful young woman, who Mary instinctively knew was pregnant, although it may not have been obvious to many people.

William introduced Nadine to his mother, and before he could say any more Mary had ushered them into the sitting room, and immediately informed them that they must be thirsty after their journey, and therefore she would make them a nice cup of tea. No sooner had they sat down than Mary was bustling out to the kitchen to make the tea, re-appearing after a minute or so to say, "Would Nadine prefer a cup of coffee? I could pop down the shop to get some coffee." Touched at being shown such kindness when she was a virtual stranger, Nadine replied, "I would very much like a cup of tea, please," although she had never drunk tea before and had no idea what it would taste like. No sooner had the tea arrived, and they were drinking it, than Mary became concerned that they were hungry, and she then was trying to determine what they would like to eat.

Eventually William managed to tell his mother what had happened since he had returned to France. Finally he uttered the words that Mary had been hoping she would hear from him since he had reappeared on the door step.

"Mum we've come back to England for good: do you know of somewhere we can stay?"

"Of course I do," his mother replied. "There is room enough for all of us in this house provided Nadine does not mind."

"But mum," said William. "Nadine is pregnant and soon she will be having a baby!"

"Yes, I know," his mother replied, beaming, "but there is still plenty of room here if Nadine would like to move in. Talk it over with her while I wash up the cups dear, and then I must go down the Village to get you something to eat."

Although Nadine's command of the English language was good, the rapid conversation between mother and son in the soft Somerset burr, meant that she had not managed to follow the whole of the conversation, and William had to explain slowly what his mother had said. When he had finished Nadine sat silently looking at him for a moment and then said, "Are you sure that is what your mother meant?"

William replied, "Why don't you ask her?"

Nadine went into the kitchen and plucked up the courage to ask Mary, "Mrs Hawkes, did you really mean it when you said that we could stay here with you? Are you sure that you don't mind?"

When her mother-in-law replied, "Of course not dear, you are part of the family now!" Nadine rushed up to her and hugged her before bursting into tears. Mary, who was unused to such displays of emotion from her own family, and still unaware of all that had happened between Nadine and her own mother, put her daughter-in-law's behaviour down to her Latin temperament, and wondered how often these displays occurred.

Once she had stemmed Nadine's flow of tears Mary announced that she was going shopping in the village, and after a brief glance at William, to see if it would be all right, Nadine asked if she could go with her. The two women set off together, and as they walked into the village Mary tried to explain to Nadine that many foodstuffs were still rationed, and until William and Nadine got their ration books they would have to get by on fish and other items that were off ration.

Already impressed by the hospitality she had been shown by her mother-in-law, Nadine soon became aware that such behaviour was the norm in Somerset. In every shop they went into, and with everyone they met in the street, Mary introduced Nadine to them as her new daughter-in-law, at the same time informing them that she would be staying in the village. Nadine noticed that without exception they all welcomed her to the village and expressed the hope that she would be very happy there. She could not help contrasting her welcome in England to the one that her fellow countrymen and women had given William when he arrived in their midst.

The following morning they quickly obtained the ration books they needed, and started to make all the other arrangements for Nadine to become a British Citizen, so that she could remain in the country. As soon as they had finished these tasks, William wasted no time in reporting to the Labour Exchange where, after he had explained the qualifications he had gained in the Army, he was informed that the GWR were looking for fitters in the loco sheds at Taunton. Remembering his previous experience when he had tried to join the railway many years before, he did not expect to be taken on, but he reported to the Foreman Fitter as instructed, knowing that if he did not do so he would not be able to claim any unemployment benefits.

The foreman checked his service records, and William had outlined his experiences in the Army with the S160s and the Austerities. The foreman looked at him for a while and then said, "We've not got S160s here any longer son, but we do get a few Austerities in from time to time so you will be the most experienced fitter that we have got on those. But it is a pity that you have not had more experience working on proper engines." (meaning GWR engines).

William replied, "But I have worked on proper engines as well: when I first started in the army I was working on Dean goods locos."

The foreman laughed and then said, "Well I'm afraid that you won't see many of those around now either, although we do get the odd one in occasionally." He then continued, "We are experiencing great difficulties in persuading skilled fitters to work on the railway, because they can earn more money in factories, where the work is not so heavy, dirty, or even so strenuous, and they are not expected to work shift patterns." The foreman then paused, and looked at William to see if he was still interested in the job, because normally it was at this point that most applicants changed their mind about working on the railway.

When he saw that William's interest remained undiminished, he glanced at William's service record again, and asked, "Were you happy working in the Army at outstations for long periods on your own, with just a fitter's mate to assist you?" William replied, "That never worried me."

For a while the foreman sat deep in thought and then said, "We are also experiencing problems in finding people who are prepared to work as relief fitters at the various sub sheds. Once you are familiar with the problems you are likely to encounter on the engines that are shedded here, would you be prepared to consider undertaking that work?"

After he was informed that it would result in extra pay, William explained, "I have just got married, and I need all the extra money that I can get, and I am not only willing to work all the overtime I can manage, and work at the subsheds, but I am happy to do shift work too." As soon as the foreman heard that, he announced, "I am prepared to take you on, provided you pass the necessary medical examination, subject of course to a three month's trial."

A few days later William received his travel warrant to travel to Swindon for his medical. After the medical examinations had been completed, and he had finished trying to identify the colours of various grimy balls of wool that had been handled by hundreds of previous applicants over the past years, he was informed that he had been passed fit, and that his foreman would be told that he was available to start work on the following Monday.

Once William had started working, Nadine quickly settled into her new surroundings. There were some things she missed, but soon she was happily drinking tea instead of coffee. She also missed her red wine which was difficult to obtain locally, and when it was available, Nadine considered it to be expensive, and of poor quality, but she soon acquired a taste for the local cider which was cheap, plentiful and delicious.

It was not long before Nadine was helping Mary by going shopping on her own, and doing some of the cooking, and housework. When they had first moved in Mary was concerned that two women in the kitchen would cause friction. After much thought, she had suggested that as well as their bedroom, and a second room, that was soon to become a nursery the couple might prefer another room that they could use as a sitting room so that William and Nadine would be alone. She also suggested that possibly it would be easier for Nadine if they used the kitchen at different times.

When Mary suggested this to Nadine she would not hear of it, saying that she felt that they were already causing Mary too much trouble. After a while, to Mary's delight, she found that they managed to work well together, although it took some time for her to get used to the amount of garlic that Nadine put into all her cooking, but she had to admit that apart from that, Nadine was a very good cook.

Mary wasted no time in writing to Mary-Ann to tell her the news that William had arrived home with his new wife, and that she was soon to be a grandmother.

PROSPEROUS TIMES?

In the area around Chadwell Heath, the first priority when the war ended was to repair the many badly damaged houses as soon as possible, when the materials that were required became available. As the programme of house repairs was nearing completion, the empty plots that Mary-Ann had noticed along the High Street and in Chadwell Heath Lane, when she had first arrived in the area, were developed, with either new houses or shops built on them

By 1948 building materials of all kinds, together with the craftsmen needed to build the houses, were no longer in short supply, and the private developers, together with the local council and the London County Council, were able not only to complete the estates that had been started before the war, but then to go on to build houses on huge new housing estates, on what had previously been open countryside. No sooner had the pre war estates been completed, than the open spaces that Mary-Ann had seen at the top of Chadwell Heath Lane when her furniture was delivered also became new housing estates.

One day as she passed the site, at the top of the lane, of one of the older houses, that had been demolished, she noticed with regret the site was being redeveloped. She recalled how only a few months previously she had paid a house visit there, and a goat that had been tethered in the front garden had broken its restraining chain and had chased her down the garden path as she was leaving. She had only just managed to shut the ramshackle gate behind her, before the goat hit it with considerable force.

The new housing developments, together with the resultant increase in the number of patients registering with them, created further demands on the service that she and her partner were trying to provide. In the end they were forced to stop taking any new patients, because they were both working up to eighteen hours a day during the winter months.

Later, as she travelled around the area she noticed that in the fields where she and her mother had watched the biplanes doing circuits and bumps a few years ago, developers were now building the largest council estate in the country, to accommodate people made homeless in the blitz on the East End of London. Even this vast building programme was insufficient to meet all the demand for new houses. Soon the former Battle of Britain airfields at Hornchurch, North Weald, and Fairlop were being built on, and so in a little over ten years the area that she had grown to know so well had changed from a semi-rural area, into a vast urban sprawl.

When the idea of the National Health Service had first been mooted, both Mary-Ann and Harry were very supportive of the idea, in spite of the misgivings expressed by many of their colleagues. When the service started in 1948, they were determined to see that they did everything they could to ensure its success.

They were completely unprepared for the huge upsurge in the demands on their time by their patients as soon as the service was available. This was due to the large number of people who now made appointments to see the doctor, because the service was free. They would previously have shrugged off a cold or other minor ailment, and waited for it to clear up, or would have used one of the many old-fashioned but very effective old wives' remedies available, or simply called into the chemist for aspirins.

Other patients expected their doctors to make house visits at all times, even for minor ailments, often in the middle of the night. This increased their workload still further. The two partners' ability to cope with these problems was not helped by a steadily increasing level of bureaucracy, which left them both wondering how much longer they would be able to cope. They discussed the possibility of taking on another partner, but on reflection considered that it was impossible on their present site, and they were unable to locate suitable premises in the immediate vicinity.

When the railways were nationalised in 1948 William, like many other people who worked on them, thought that things would improve. It was not long before William and his colleagues in the industry became disillusioned. For a while the procedures that had been successfully followed for generations continued, and only some job titles were changed.

He, along with others, had laughed at the practice of the old GWR never to spend a penny if it could be avoided. For example, they had often wondered how cost effective it was to send broken broom handles to Swindon so that they could be turned into shafts for hammers. Now they were appalled at the wastage that had started to occur; it seemed that changes were introduced with no thought given to the probable cost, or even the effectiveness of the change.

One such example was the decision to change the system that identified the shed that a particular locomotive was allocated to. The GWR had a system where each shed was given an easily identified code which was stencilled on the frame of the loco, usually just behind the buffer beam. This was a cheap and easy way to identify the home shed of that particular engine. Under the old system the code for Taunton shed was TN, but under the new system it became 83B and this number was carried on a cast plate fitted to the smoke box door. Thousands of the plates were cast to cover every shed throughout the system, and many hundreds were later thrown away when locos were allocated to another shed.

A cast number plate was also fitted to the smoke box door, which could not be seen on express locomotives when the reporting number frame was carried, but this was supposed to be an improvement on the GWR practice of painting the number on the buffer beam where it could easily be seen. The livery of some of the coaching stock was changed over a very short period from chocolate and cream, to rhubarb and custard: later to maroon, and finally back to chocolate and cream again.

At the same time the colours of the locomotives were changed from Brunswick green, to blue, then to black, and finally back to Brunswick green again. While this was going on the fitters were working on locos out in the open in pouring rain, sometimes in freezing conditions because there was no room for them to work under cover. Another problem was that the overhead lighting in the shed was so poor that they had to work by the light cast by flare-lamps even when it was daylight. The coaling facilities also needed to be improved, but there appeared to be no money to spend on essential work of this kind.

On the 18th January 1948 William became a father for the first time when Nadine gave birth to a baby girl, and they named her Danielle. When Nadine went round the local shops with her daughter for the first time on her own after the birth of the baby, she could not understand why most of the people she met would persist in giving the baby silver coins. When she arrived home Mary explained to her that many people thought that by following this custom they would bring the baby good luck.

As soon as he was able to do so, William decided it would be better for all of them if he purchased a small car, and he eventually obtained a second hand pre war Morris Eight from a garage in the village. Looking at the car standing outside the house while William was at work, Nadine decided that they could make better use of the car if she learned to drive it, and then she could take the family out while her husband was at work. After a number of driving lessons from William she passed her driving test at the first attempt.

For Mary this period was the happiest time in her life since before her Bill had been killed. She found that Nadine was more than just a daughter-in-law, she was also a friend and a companion, who did not appear to mind when Mary fussed over the baby like every other doting grandmother. Nadine for her part was grateful for any advice or help that Mary gave her. Both William and Nadine were also glad that Mary never seemed to mind baby sitting for them whenever they wanted to go out together. Their happiness was complete when Nadine gave birth to a second daughter in April 1951, and they decided to call her Louise.

On a bitterly cold morning in January 1955 Nadine was getting both the children dressed, for when they were ready she intended to drop Danielle off at the school, and then go shopping with Mary, taking Louise with her in the pushchair. To Nadine's surprise when the children were ready Mary said to her, "Do you mind if I don't come with you today dear? I'm not feeling very well." When Nadine asked if she should call the Doctor Mary said, "No, it's all right, I've just got a pain in my arm, and I feel rather tired, I didn't have a very good night's sleep."

Without thinking any more about the matter Nadine set off to drop Danielle at the school, and then do her shopping. Arriving back at the house, as Nadine was opening the front door she glanced in the window of the sitting room and saw Mary sitting in her favourite armchair, and was delighted to think that she was resting for a while. After she had put away the shopping, she put Louise down for her morning sleep, and then made a cup of tea for herself, and another for Mary.

When she entered the room Nadine was surprised when there was no immediate response from Mary. Her surprise turned to concern when she could not rouse her, and finally turned to shock when she suddenly realised that Mary was dead..

For the first time in her life, Nadine, who until now had always thought that she was level-headed and capable of dealing with any emergency, suddenly panicked. After she had calmed down a little, she realised that her first task was to telephone the doctor, who arrived within a few minutes of her call. After a brief examination he confirmed that Mary was dead. The doctor then tried to calm Nadine, who in his opinion appeared to be in a state of shock, so that she could attend to Louise who had been woken by the noise, and was crying upstairs.

While Nadine attended to her daughter, the doctor made a number of telephone calls, on the telephone that he knew had only recently been installed in the house, at the railways expense, to enable them to contact William in an emergency. When Nadine came down stairs with Louise, the doctor told her of the arrangements he had made for Mary's body to be removed, and then explained that as this was a sudden death, there would have to be a post mortem. While she was waiting for Mary's body to be collected Nadine rang the loco shed and asked to speak to William. At first the foreman fitter did not recognise her voice, and informed her, "I'm sorry, madam, but William cannot take private telephone calls at work."

After Nadine explained what had happened he apologised, and told her, "William has been sent out to Minehead, and is working on a loco in the shed there." He then told her, "I will get a message to your husband without delay, and arrange for him to return to Bishops Lydeard, by the next available train. I will also tell him there will be no need for him to return to the shed to book off duty. If he has not completed the work on his job sheet I will arrange for another fitter to be sent to complete the work."

Thanking him profusely for his help Nadine settled down to await William's return. While she was doing so she rang her sister-in-law, only to find that she was still out of the surgery on her house calls. Leaving a message with Harry, she asked Mary-Ann to ring her as soon as she returned. When her sister-in-law rang back forty-five minutes later Nadine tried to break the news of Mary's death as gently as possible to her. There was a long silence at the other end of the phone before Mary-Ann, spoke in a very husky voice.

"Thank you, Nadine, for ringing. I will leave as soon as possible after evening surgery has finished, and travel down overnight. I hope to arrive first thing tomorrow morning."

Later that morning, as William was hurrying up the road from the station, he met the doctor, who after offering his condolences, informed William, "I think that when the post mortem is held tomorrow, it will confirm my opinion, that your mother died of a heart attack."

When the family awoke the following morning, and looked out of the window, they saw a new blue Austin Cambridge saloon car parked in the road, outside the house. William immediately realised that his sister had arrived, and after rescuing her from the cold car Nadine revived her with some soup that she had warmed up that had been left over from the night before, when neither of them seemed able to face any food at all.

As Nadine started to get Danielle ready to go to school Mary-Ann tried to find out from Nadine and William exactly what had happened the previous day. Before long Mary-Ann realised that her sister-in-law was still in a state of shock, and so she arranged to take her niece to school. Before she left, Mary-Ann gained the impression that for some reason William's presence was disturbing Nadine, so she suggested that it might be better if he returned to work. As she left the house she promised that she would return shortly, to help Nadine with the arrangements for the funeral.

After Mary-Ann had left Danielle at the school, before returning to Nadine's home, she visited the doctor's surgery. After she had introduced herself, the doctor offered Mary-Ann his condolences, and then said, "I am pleased to meet you at last, I have heard so much about you from your mother." After they had exchanged further pleasantries Mary-Ann found out that the post mortem was to be held at 10am that morning.

"May I visit you later to discuss the results?" she asked.

"Of course. Come back here and meet me at 11am," he replied. "And I see no reason why your family should not start to make the arrangements for the funeral, because I feel certain that there will not be any problems."

While she was helping Nadine before returning to meet the doctor again, Mary-Ann had a chance to find out what was so worrying her sister-in-law. Nadine confessed her guilty feelings.

"If only I hadn't gone out shopping and left Mary alone! And I should have insisted on calling the doctor, even though she said 'no'. And if I hadn't allowed her to do so much for the children, she might still be alive!"

When she returned after visiting the doctor, Mary-Ann was able to reassure her sister-in-law.

"It has been confirmed that my mother suffered a massive heart attack. Her death was instantaneous and she didn't suffer in any way. There was nothing that anyone could have done to prevent it. We must be grateful it was so peaceful."

That evening Mary-Ann left to return home knowing that all the necessary arrangements had been made and the funeral would be held at 11am on the following Wednesday with the Rev. Hamilton Jones conducting the service. As she left she informed William and Nadine that she would be returning late on the following Tuesday evening, and they promised to wait up and to have a room ready for her when she arrived.

On the morning of the service, although it was a bitterly cold day the sun was shining brightly. The church was full. Many of those present, the family realised, were villagers who had known Mary all their lives, but there were many others they did not recognise. It was only after the service and the internment that they learned that they were many of Mary's colleagues who had worked with her in the shirt factory, and still remembered her, although she had left almost ten years previously.

Nadine had arranged a small buffet for the mourners back at the house, and after everyone had departed, their solicitor read the contents of Mary's will to the family. Apart from two small bequests to her grandchildren, Mary had arranged for the balance of her estate to be divided equally between her two children. He then started to explain that as part of the estate consisted of the house, the executor would have to arrange to sell the house to ensure that the bequest was properly apportioned.

Suddenly William realised that he and Nadine would have to leave the house in which they had both spent so many wonderful moments since arriving on the door step, following their unhappy experiences in France. It was at this moment that his sister dropped her bombshell.

Looking straight at Mr Adams, the solicitor, she said, "I do not wish to see my brother and his family ejected from the house." They all looked at her. She continued, "I have become increasingly unhappy with the workload I am expected to cope with, and the increasing bureaucracy that is being experienced by all doctors in this country. I have corresponded for many years with a friend I knew at medical school, who emigrated to

Canada and has prospered, without working the excessive hours I am expected to do. When I told him of the conditions I was working under he wrote asking me if I would like to join him as a partner at his practise in Winnipeg. I have hesitated to accept his offer until now because I was concerned about mother's health." She concluded, "I have checked during the past week to see if the offer is still open, and having learned that it is, I shall be leaving this country and joining him in Canada as soon as all the necessary arrangements can be made."

When Mary-Ann finished there was a stunned silence in the room, with the solicitor looking at William for his reaction to the news. He was as surprised as everyone else in the room.

Recovering quickly from his shock William said, "Although I am very grateful for my sister's kind suggestion, I shall be unhappy if her wishes are followed, because she will not obtain the benefit from mother's will that was intended. If that happened, mother would never forgive me!" After a slight pause he looked straight at the solicitor and added, "Can you suggest another way to resolve this problem please?"

The solicitor, who had not considered the possibility of this situation arising, had to think quickly, and finally suggested the only possible solution to the problem.

"You could have the house valued and then you, William, could purchase Mary-Ann's share of the house, with the remainder of your legacy."

William looked briefly towards his wife to see if she agreed with the proposal. When she indicated that she did, he instructed Mr Adams to proceed with the arrangements.

At the beginning of May, Mary-Ann telephoned, and when Nadine answered the phone, asked if she could stay with them the following weekend. Nadine said that they would be delighted to see her. Mary-Ann then confirmed that she would be arriving on Friday evening.

On the following Friday afternoon when Nadine was on her way to collect Danielle from school, Nadine was surprised to see her sister-in-law walking through the village carrying a large suitcase. Before she was able to speak to her, Mary-Ann had entered Mr Adam's office.

Later that same afternoon there was a knock at the door and when Nadine opened it Mary-Ann was standing on the door step with the large suit case, but she did not appear to have arrived in her car. As Nadine prepared the by now customary cup of tea that she gave to all her visitors, she asked why there was no car.

"Oh," said Mary-Ann, "I've got lots of news to tell you, but can I wait until my brother arrives, otherwise I will have to repeat it all over again!"

Knowing that William would be home shortly Nadine decided she would have to be patient. So it was not until after they had eaten their meal, Mary-Ann had helped her brother with the dishes, and Nadine had bathed the children, and tucked them up in bed, that Nadine was able to tell William that his sister had got some very important news to tell them, before he settled down in front of the television set.

It was then that Mary-Ann shared her news with them.

"I have just wound up all my affairs in England and I shall be leaving for Canada next Tuesday!"

When Nadine exclaimed, "That means that we shall not see you again!"

Mary-Ann replied, "Not only do I hope that you will be able to come over for a holiday some time, but I intend to return to this country to visit you as soon as it is practical."

After sitting in silence for several minutes, Nadine could no longer contain her curiosity and suddenly she said to Mary-Ann, "Why did you go to Mr Adams' office this afternoon?"

Mary-Ann looked surprised that Nadine knew about her visit but in a quiet voice she informed her, "I went in to say goodbye, to thank him for all his help in the past, and to give him my new address in Canada."

During the weekend Mary-Ann attempted to visit those friends in the village who remembered her from the time she lived there, and on Sunday evening she invited as many of them as could come, to join her and her family for a last convivial evening in the Lethbridge Arms. It was during the course of the evening William learned what long memories some of the locals had, when they asked him if Canadians also thought that cider was apple juice. From the laughter it was obvious that many of them still remembered carrying Grant up to bed.

The following Tuesday morning Mary Ann left the village by train to catch her flight to Canada from Heathrow.

RETIRING TIME

During all their early married life, William and his growing family had spent their summer holidays at home, often going on day trips to the coast, the zoo, or to other local attractions. Sometimes they went for walks or picnics in the Quantocks, always taking Mary with them.

Following Mary's death William realised that the whole family needed a 'proper' holiday. Now that their financial situation had improved a little, he decided that the time had come to take them away for a week. On the recommendation of a work-mate, they booked a week's holiday in a B&B farmhouse in North Wales at a place called Penrhyndeudraeth.

On the Saturday morning at the start of their holiday they left the house before 6am, and apart from a short break around midday for a meal, they were driving the whole day. It had started to pour with rain after they left the town of Craven Arms and had not stopped since, so by 5pm the children were becoming fretful, tired and they both needed to go to the toilet urgently. They stopped for another short break, but by this time Nadine was beginning to have grave doubts that they would arrive at their destination that night, in spite of William's assurance that they were almost there. When they set off again Nadine decided to sit in the back of the car to comfort the children and try to get them to sleep for a little while. William would have to drive for the remainder of the journey.

Dusk was starting to fall as they approached Maentwrog, and William saw a sign indicating that they should turn left for Penrhyndeudraeth. What he did not notice in the gathering gloom was the small sign underneath which indicated that it was a toll road. As they drove along the road

Nadine, who was only half awake, heard what she thought was a terrible clanking noise coming from the car. When she voiced her concern William laughed and pointed at the long goods train pulled by yet another Dean goods engine that they were slowly overtaking as it travelled on the railway line alongside the road. His laughter soon ceased when they had to stop at the toll booth, where he had to struggle to find change to pay for the privilege of using the single track road.

Arriving in what he thought was the centre of the village, William stopped and asked a lady who was waiting to cross the road, for directions to their destination. He showed her the rather grubby piece of paper with the address of their destination on it, because he was unable to pronounce the name of the farm. After a brief glance at it she told him in a lilting Welsh accent, "Turn right, go straight over the cross roads up the hill, and then take the second turning on the left after the railway crossing."

By now it was dark and after they had gone about half a mile down the lane William suddenly realised that there was a tractor proceeding down the lane in front of them with no lights on. There was no way that he could overtake it, so he followed it for a mile and a half until it came to a sudden standstill without any warning. When the driver switched off the engine, and jumped down from the tractor he seemed surprised that a car had followed him into the farmyard. He walked back to their car, and as he did so William lowered the window and asked, "Can you direct me to…" and then he paused as he tried to work out how to pronounce the name on the scrap of paper.

"Ysgyfarnogod Farm," said the farmer, and when William nodded and said. "I think so!" the farmer said, "You've arrived! You must be Mr & Mrs Hawkes then. We were wondering when you were going to arrive. Wait a moment, and I'll move the tractor so that you can park near the house." As soon as the car pulled up in front of the house, the front door opened and Mrs Evans came out with a shawl over her head and shoulders to keep the worst of the rain off. She hastened them into the house in the dry, while Mr Evans and William collected the suitcases from the boot of the car.

After showing them to their room Mrs Evans made them a welcoming cup of tea. Nadine knew that William liked a strong brew and was worried that he might make an observation about the strength of the cuppa he had just been offered. Later that week they were to learn that the name of that brand of tea was 'Golden Stream' which they considered to be very apt. While they drank their tea William apologised for their late arrival and explained some of the problems they had encountered on their trip. As he was finishing his tea, and his explanation, Mrs Evans served up a very welcoming meal of roast lamb and new potatoes, saying, "You must be hungry after that journey."

After they had finished their meal, Nadine put the children to bed, and as soon as they were asleep they made their apologies to their hosts and went to bed themselves. As Nadine lay in bed she found that she was unable to sleep because of a persistent dripping sound. After lying awake for some time she decided to investigate. Switching on the bed side lamp, she got out of bed and had only taken a few steps across the room in her bare feet when she became aware that she was standing on a very wet piece of lino. Tracing the dampness back to its source she found that the water was dripping onto the window sill where it had formed a large puddle which had eventually overflowed, and had run down the wall, and across the floor.

Trying to rouse William without waking the children, who were in the same room, she whispered, "There's water pouring into the room!" to which William, still only half awake, replied, "We're not going to drown are we? So come back to bed." This response brought him a clout around the head from Nadine that finally woke him up, and he decided that the only way that he was going to get any further sleep would be if he investigated the problem.

His first thought was to wake Mr & Mrs Evans, but walking towards the door he noticed a large old-fashioned china chamber pot underneath the bed. Holding it aloft in triumph he marched over to the window sill and placed it in position to catch the drips. As he tried to get back in to bed Nadine was whispering to him, "You can't leave that there!"

"Why not?" replied William. "It's more use there than under the bed!" She then refused to allow him back in bed until he had dried his feet.

By the time they finished their breakfast the following morning the rain had stopped, but it was very blustery and overcast, certainly not warm enough to take the children down to the beach, which was the main reason for bringing them on holiday.

Instead they made their way to Beddgelert, and after they had parked the car they walked round the village for a while, window shopping. Finally, arriving at the edge of the village, they started to walk along what they thought was a footpath, which they later discovered was the trackbed of the former Welsh Highland Railway, that had closed almost twenty years earlier. Standing on the trackbed just a few feet above the Afon Glaslyn, they were fascinated by the torrent of water that was pouring through the narrow gorge after the heavy rain of the previous twenty-four hours.

Because the sun had still not appeared, in the afternoon they drove into Porthmadog. After a snack and a drink, William followed Nadine and the children who were window shopping, as they strolled along the main road. Suddenly in the distance he noticed a long low stone building and a four foot high wall adjacent to the building which ran alongside the road for some distance. He could see no sign to indicate what the building was, and after telling Nadine where he was going, he wandered over the river bridge towards the building, so that he could take a closer look. All the doors and windows in it were boarded up, but peering over the wall he saw that there were a number of narrow gauge railway tracks behind the wall, and alongside the low platform at the rear of the building.

Although the rails were rusty, grass was growing between the tracks, and it was obvious that no trains had run along the line for some time, there were some signs of recent activity. Most of the carriages that were standing in the station area, for that is what the building was, had been covered with tarpaulins, and some of the bushes and shrubs that had been growing between and alongside the tracks had been cleared. Unfortunately he could not see anyone to ask what was going on, and there were no name boards remaining on the station to indicate to which railway the site had formerly belonged. Intrigued by his discovery William walked back to rejoin his family, deep in thought.

The weather turned out to be warm and sunny for the remainder of their holiday, and most of their time was spent on the almost deserted Black Rock sands, where they found that they could drive the car onto the beach, and leave it there for the whole day. Driving each way between their B&B and the beach during that week William spotted other features that he assumed, in the absence of any other information, belonged to the same railway company. The disused level crossing on the hill as they climbed out of Penrhyndeudraeth, the bridge over the lane to the farmhouse where they were staying, and what appeared to be another disused station alongside the main road out of Portmadog.

On the last night of their holiday after they had eaten their meal, while Nadine was putting the children to bed, William, still intrigued by his discovery, announced that he was going out for a short walk. As she waited for the children to go to sleep, Nadine looked out of the bedroom window and saw William strolling down the lane until he stopped just short of the railway bridge. She was surprised to see that after pausing for a moment he scrambled up the embankment, and then walked along the trackbed until he was out of sight.

When William had been walking along the trackbed for about twenty minutes, he suddenly became aware of the smell of newly baked bread. Coming out of the cutting he noticed yet another disused station, and suddenly realised that at the end of the dilapidated platform was the level crossing he had driven over many times during the past week. As William turned to retrace his steps the owner came out of the bakery situated on the opposite side of the narrow lane that ran alongside the trackbed.

"Good evening," he said to William as he slowly walked past.

Stopping to pass the time of day with the man, William thought perhaps at last he could learn something about this railway line, but the information that he was given was not encouraging. The baker told him, "The line belongs to the Ffestiniog Railway, and it used to bring slate down from Blaenau Ffestiniog to Portmadog, but nothing has travelled along the line since before the war when the people running it went broke." Pausing for a moment while he drew on his cigarette, he continued, "There's talk of some foreigners (by which he meant English people), from Birmingham I think, who are trying to re-open the line. If they manage to do so it will be a complete waste of time, you mark my words – there's no demand for slate these days."

Having spent much longer talking to the baker than he had intended, when William arrived back at the farmhouse it was dark, and Nadine was convinced by then that he had managed to get lost. As they sat talking before they went to bed William explained what had been on his mind during the past week. He then told her of the information he had been given that evening, and finished the conversation by saying to Nadine, "It seems such a pity that they will never be able to achieve their aims, because at least they are trying to re-open a railway line, whereas in England all they seem to be interested in is closing them." Some years later William was to be proved spectacularly wrong.

The next morning the family set off on their trip back to Somerset.

Three years later, in 1958, Mary-Ann wrote to inform William and Nadine that she had married the doctor she had been working with in Canada, and they would be coming to England for a short break in the fall.

That same year the first of the new diesel locomotives to be built under the much vaunted 'Modernisation Plan' came into regular service on the West of England main line. Before long the sight of them hurrying past Taunton shed with trains to and from Cornwall, and the other intermediate locations in the West of England, became an every day occurrence. As the number of diesel engines increased, unfortunately their reliability seemed if anything to get worse.

In 1960 William was sent on a course and when he had completed it, he was passed out as a qualified diesel fitter. This qualification did William very little good, because management had decided that Taunton was to remain a steam shed, which meant they were not allocated any spares even to complete minor repairs on the new locos. One day a new diesel engine limped into Taunton Station and William was summoned to see if he could locate the fault and rectify it so that the train could continue on its journey. He located the fault and found that he needed a ¼ inch BSF set screw to rectify the problem which, of course, he did not have. He then had no alternative but to declare the engine a failure, and a Hall class loco badly in need of an intermediate overhaul, was summoned from the shed, and coupled to the train to enable it to complete its journey.

After that time William tried to ensure that he did not fail any steam locos if he could avoid it, robbing components from other less fortunate members of the same class that were in the shed, in order to keep the loco running. He knew that if he failed any steam loco, and it was sent to Swindon for overhaul or repair, it would be scrapped. Once again he could not understand the thinking by management who decided that a small sum, often less than £200, could not be spent on a steam loco that could, with luck, result in it giving a further ten year's service. Meanwhile, thousands of pounds were being spent on new diesel locos, some of which were so unreliable because of inherent design faults, that they were scrapped less that ten years after they were built.

In the summer of 1960 the first three diesel shunting locos, later known as the Class 03, were allocated to Taunton shed to work the various goods yards in the Taunton area. At the same time the only piece of equipment that was sent to the shed to help with the maintenance of the new equipment – a battery charger! – arrived. The theory was that the engines could be started by compressed air from a cylinder on the loco that was filled from a hand pump fitted to the loco. This would turn over the engine and start it. Frequently this did not work and the shed staff were treated to the spectacle of a steam loco towing the shunters along the approach road to the shed in order to bump start them.

The next diesel locomotives to be allocated to the shed were the more powerful 350HP shunting engines, which later became known as the Class 08. These suffered similar starting problems, but had to be towed backwards to bump start them.

Later that year the first DMUs (Diesel Multiple Units) arrived to work the branch line services to Minehead. In the winter months these units worked two round trips to Minehead on a Sunday and then stood in the bay platform at Taunton station until the time came for them to be prepared for the 8.10am service on Monday morning. Attempts to start the set then would often result in a flat battery, because the batteries were dependant on dynamos on the axles of the units to charge them. When this happened, a steam loco had to be coupled to the front of the railcar and the unit towed to Bishops Lydeard station, and back again to generate enough charge in the batteries to attempt to start the engines again.

To overcome this problem, the engines on the DMUs were left ticking over all night. The units were based at Bristol and had to be returned there for any service work, including refuelling, to be carried out. During 1964 more and more of the steam engines that had been allocated to Taunton, including some that had been based there for many years, were sent away to be scrapped, and before long the entire site began to look like a ghost town. It came as no surprise to most of the railway men of all grades who were employed in the shed when they were informed that they would be made redundant when the shed closed in 1965. William was more fortunate than many of the others because he was offered a job as a fitter in the new diesel sheds at either Bristol or Cardiff.

Danielle, William's eldest daughter had started work in 1963, after leaving school as soon as she was fifteen years old. She worked for the same firm, but not in the same factory, where her grandmother had worked for so many years. The factory was situated in the village, and so she did not have the problem that her grandmother had experienced of travelling into Taunton each day.

When Danielle had returned home after her interview and announced that she would be starting the following

Monday, she casually informed her mother that the firm had plenty of vacancies for machinists.

Nadine knew that it was only a matter of time before William would be made redundant, and they had often discussed what they would do if this happened, without reaching any firm decision. Although William thought that he might be offered work elsewhere on the railway, they had agreed that as he had only ten more years to work before he retired he should attempt to find another job locally. The reason for arriving at this decision, was simply because they considered that it was pointless to sell the house, and uproot the family from the area, knowing that when William retired, they would return to the area they had all grown to know, and love so well.

When William returned from work one evening, Nadine, who had been thinking about this problem all day, told him what Danielle had said.

Remembering the time they had spent in France when he had been unable to obtain work, she knew that William would not be happy with her suggestion, if he thought that the family were dependant upon her efforts in order to keep themselves fed and clothed. At the same time she knew he would not want to go on the dole.

"Perhaps," she suggested, "I should take a job at the factory for a short while, so that we can could build up a small nest egg to ensure, that, if you are made redundant, there would be less urgency for you to get any job simply to provide sufficient money to meet our needs."

When she had raised the matter with him, although he could understand her reasoning, William was reluctant to even consider the idea at first. He was concerned that Nadine would be unable to cope with working in the factory all day and then the housework when she returned home in the evening. After she assured him that it would not be a problem, and that the girls would help her, he agreed to let her go along to the factory for an interview.

But his final words to her on the subject were, "If I think that it is too much for you, I want you to promise me that you will stop work immediately." Nadine agreed, knowing that if she did not, there was no way William would allow her even to start.

When William was made redundant, he was amongst the first to arrive at the Labour Exchange to look for a new job, unlike so many of his workmates who waited until their redundancy money had gone before they started to search for other work. When he arrived at the Labour Exchange he was informed that a local dairy company had a vacancy for a lorry driver, to collect milk from local farms and deliver it to the dairy. William went straight to his prospective new employer, and after he had told the manager of the type of lorries he had driven before the war, and the area that he had covered, he was asked if he could start the following morning. Although the wages were less than he had been receiving on the railway, and it meant he would have to make a very early start each morning, William knew that they could get by even if, as he hoped, Nadine decided not to work at the shirt factory any longer.

When William returned home after his interview Nadine was still at work of, course, and he decided that he could not wait until she returned home in the evening. He decided that he would meet her and Danielle as they left the factory in the evening, to tell them his good news. He was a little disappointed when Nadine suggested that perhaps she should continue to work for a while, in case he could not settle down in his new job, due to the early starts, late finishes and the possibility that he might have to work seven days a week if a relief driver was not available. As Nadine pointed out, cows need milking seven days a week: realising that as usual his wife was right, William reluctantly accepted the situation.

William soon settled in his job, and found that he was constantly reminded of the sights, the sounds, and the scenery, that he remembered so well, from the past, when that appeared before him again. So much remained largely unaltered since the carefree days before the war, as he drove around the Brendon and Quantock hills. One morning, possibly because he was earlier, or the train was later, than usual, as he approached the level crossing gates at Williton Station he found them closed against him.

A DMU was standing in the UP platform, waiting for the down train to arrive. As he waited he noticed how many things around the station had changed since he had driven a lorry into the now deserted goods shed at the station, to collect material for the Doniford camp site some thirty years earlier.

The sidings were deserted. The rusty rails, with grass growing high between them showed that no trains had shunted there for some time. The once busy goods shed was now locked and boarded up, and weeds were growing in the gutters of the various buildings on the site, and small shrubs grew out of the walls of some of the station buildings. The passing loop had been shortened, presumably in an attempt to save money, and where once there had been about fifteen members of staff working at the station there now appeared to be only one, the signalman who presumably had a relief to cover the remainder of the day so the staffing level appeared to have been reduced to two.

Some of the old standards appeared to have been retained however. The permanent way appeared to be in perfect condition, with not a weed in sight in the four foot, and indeed one section of track appeared to have been recently re-laid. The windows of the signal box still gleamed as they had always done in the past where they had been cleaned by the signalman when he came on duty each morning. As he watched, William could see him now, busy buffing the highly polished floor in the signal box, until the sound of the klaxon horn on the approaching DMU sent him scurrying down the steps of the signal box, to collect the token from the driver of the incoming train.

After a few minutes of frantic activity by the signalman, both trains departed and a very thoughtful William was allowed to proceed on his journey, when the gates opened. While he had been waiting at the crossing his mind had flashed back to the scenes he had witnessed in Wales, and once again he felt that he would like to be involved with railways again. He soon dismissed the idea because he knew that he could not get up to North Wales to help with the restoration of the railway line on a regular basis.

The constant stream of boyfriends that his eldest daughter seemed to attract was a source of constant irritation and annoyance to William. Apart from her inability to arrive home at night when her father had asked her to, she seemed to attract all the mods, rockers, drop outs, no hopers and fall outs from, and members of, unknown rock groups. On one memorable occasion Danielle's latest boyfriend had arrived early, and had been shown into the sitting room by Nadine while he waited for Danielle, who was still getting ready, and was late as usual. William awoke from his afternoon armchair nap, and still only half awake stared in absolute horror and disbelief at the apparition in front of him, who had hair down to his shoulders, and then exclaimed, "What the hell is that supposed to be? Is it a boy or a girl?" After this encounter that particular boyfriend did not reappear on the scene again, and Danielle stopped bringing her boyfriends home, because after a third degree from her father they did not want to see her again.

One Saturday morning as he drove his lorry through the village on the way back to the milk depot, William thought he saw his eldest daughter walking arm in arm with a man down Mount Street. But as the man seemed, well, almost respectable, he decided that he must be mistaken, until he looked in the nearside wing mirror of the lorry as he passed them, and found that he was not. That evening he waited up with Nadine until Danielle arrived home, late as usual. As always she popped her head round the door of the sitting room before she went upstairs, to tell her folks that she was home. Before she could close the door and disappear upstairs her father said,

"Well?"

Coming back into the room Danielle replied, "Well, what?"

"Who was that fellow I saw you walking down the road with today?" William asked.

With a sigh Danielle replied, "Dad, that is the man I love very much, that I want to marry, and he is very nice."

This was the first indication he had received that his daughter, who was only twenty years old, wanted to get married, although he noticed with some concern that Nadine did not seem as surprised as he was.

Recovering from his shock, William said, "If he is so special why have you not brought him home to meet us?"

"Because when I bring my boyfriends home," his daughter replied, "You give them the third degree, and you frighten them away, and I am determined that you are not going to do that to Brian!"

Nadine could see that her daughter was close to tears, and she was determined that this dispute should not result in her daughter leaving home, and refusing to return, as she had done with her own mother. She stepped quickly between them and said, "Danielle, please bring Brian home to see us. Your father seemed quite impressed with him when he saw him today, and I promise you he will not interrogate him."

Then she turned to William and said sharply, "Will you?"

Startled by his wife's show of anger William agreed, and it was only when Danielle had gone to bed, and her parents sat up long into the night discussing the matter, that Nadine made William realise just how close he had come to not seeing his eldest daughter again. When he met his future son-in-law, Brian, at last, he found out that not only was he was a teacher at a local secondary school, but he was also a railway enthusiast. At last, thought William, she has found a fellow with some sense, although whether Brian would be able to keep his somewhat headstrong daughter under control he had grave doubts.

Nadine then pointed out it was just as well that she had not left work, because they now had a wedding to save for, although as the happy couple were saving hard to buy a house it appeared that they might have some time to wait before they incurred that expense.

It was just as well, for the sake of William's sanity, that his youngest daughter was unlike her sister. She was much quieter, an avid reader, and when she did not have her nose in a book she was involved with the village Drama Group. She tended to go about with a group of friends of her own age of both sexes. When she left school she went to work for a short time in the local Post Office, before deciding that she wanted to become a nurse, and she started her training in Musgrove Park Hospital.

In 1970 William, like everyone else in the village, heard the not unexpected news that the railway branch line to Minehead was to close. There were of course the inevitable appeals against the decision but eventually it was decided that the last trains would run on the 2nd January 1971. Like many others William and Nadine caught one of these trains (there were three of them) from Bishops Lydeard and travelled down the line to Minehead, returning late that evening to the village.

Shortly after the line closed, Brian told William that a report had been prepared by a working party set up to investigate the possibility of re-opening the Branch line to Minehead. A meeting was to be held at the Black Horse Hotel in Taunton, on Friday 7th May to discuss these proposals, and to see if a group of volunteers could be formed to assist with the running of the Railway.

Persuaded by his future son-in-law to attend, William listened to the discussion, and although he considered that they had not got a hope in hell of ever re-opening the line, he voted for the proposals and paid the two pound membership fee for the first year. Brian became involved shortly afterwards in track clearance and other work along the line. William still considered that it was an impossible dream, and although he kept in touch with the problems the volunteers were encountering in their attempts to reopen the line, both from Brian, and also through the local press, he was not directly involved in the numerous tasks that were being carried out by volunteers in anticipation of its re-opening.

William had thought about continuing to work in full time employment after he was sixty-five years old in order to supplement both his state pension, and the small pension he received from the railway. When he approached retirement age in 1974 Nadine pointed out to him that she was about to lose her job at the shirt factory because it would shortly be closing, and that she would get a small sum of money when she was made redundant. Danielle had married her Brian and was living in Minehead where Brian was teaching, and Louise was living in the nurses home. Now, she told him, they could for the first time in their lives spend all their time together, without the need to worry about other people's problems.

Nadine pointed out that if he wanted to pursue a hobby he could always use the garden shed he had built, to produce a range of wooden garden furniture similar to the items he had made for their own garden, and which their visitors always admired. He could then sell them to supplement their income if he wanted to do so.

Unable once again to argue against Nadine's logic, William retired two days after his sixty-fifth birthday.

PASTIMES

William and Nadine had decided that when the time came that William retired, and she had been made redundant from the shirt factory they would, for the first time in their lives go away on their own for a fortnight's holiday. They also decided that they would attempt to visit many of the places they had been to with the family in North Wales over ten years ago. Now that they were no longer restricted to starting and finishing their holidays at weekends, they decided to leave on a Wednesday morning.

Remembering their previous experience they left early, but found that now the motorway had opened their travelling time was much less, and after a leisurely journey they found a roadside pub near Corris where they decided to stay for the night. They were made very welcome, the food was excellent, and their room comfortable, so the following morning they decided to stay there for the remainder of their holiday, and use it as a base to get to the other centres they planned to visit.

William could not resist the opportunity to visit the Ffestiniog railway several times, and he was both surprised and impressed at the progress that had been made since their last visit. A carefree fourteen days were spent visiting many of the other preserved narrow-gauge railway lines in the area, as well as using his privilege pass to travel on the BR Cambrian Coast line, and the Vale of Rheidol Line. They also took the opportunity to enjoy a number of long walks, including once again the walks along the former trackbed through the Aberglaslyn pass, and also along the former railway trackbed between Barmouth and Dolgellau on the southern bank of the estuary of the Afon Wnion. All too soon it was time to return home.

When William started on the return journey to Somerset he had even less to say than he normally did as he drove along. Nadine soon realised that something was disturbing him and she set about trying to find out what was going through his mind. Eventually she found that he was disappointed that he had ever doubted the abilities of the many volunteers that he had seen working during the past fortnight, and that he was more determined than ever to take part in voluntary work of that kind. But as he pointed out to Nadine it was impossible because he could not afford to travel that distance on a regular basis. As he said, "The idea was that we would spend a lot more time together than we have managed to do in the past, when I retired, and if I went away for some weekends or for a week or a fortnight at a time, that would not be fair to you."

Touched at his concern, Nadine thought about the matter for some time and eventually she said, "Well don't think that you can stay in the house getting under my feet every day, and if you still want to do that kind of work when we get home, why not have a word with Brian? He told me they are desperate for volunteers on the West Somerset Railway. You would be able to give much more time to helping them, because you can get down to the local station at any time, and you will not be wasting a lot of time and money travelling to and from Wales each time. I have no doubt that you will find yourself working with many people that you know, whereas if you travel to Wales, when you start, you will be working amongst strangers."

It was now William's turn to remain deep in thought for a time, and eventually he repeated what he had said before, "But it would still mean that I would be leaving you on your own for long periods when we have decided to spend more time together."

To which Nadine instantly replied, "What makes you think that by going down there you would be leaving me on my own? You're not going to get away from me that easily – has it not occurred to you that I might be interested in coming along as well: and they need women to help too, you know!"

Surprised at her outburst, but at the same time unable to counter the logic of her arguments, William promised that he would think the matter over.

The following Sunday morning after he had collected the newspaper from the newsagent, and eaten the full English breakfast Nadine had cooked for him, William retreated into his workshop at the end of the garden to start work on the first of the many garden benches for which he had received orders. It was a fine, warm, sunny morning, and as William set about measuring and cutting the wood for the project, he heard the unmistakable sound of the whistle of a GWR steam locomotive through the open door.

At first he ignored this distraction and carried on with his work, but when the sound was repeated several times his curiosity was aroused, and he decided that he had to go down to the station to find out what was happening. Slipping on his jacket, he called out to tell Nadine where he was going, at the same time checking what time lunch would be served. Interested in the railway William may be, but it definitely took second place to Nadine's Sunday lunch.

Arriving at the station, William was surprised at the amount of activity that was taking place. In the distance he saw a small ex GWR pannier tank locomotive moving slowly towards him drawing forward a rake of coaching stock and some goods wagons. As the engine arrived alongside him it came to a standstill and a very familiar face that he recognised from the days when he had been working at Taunton shed, peered out from the cab of the engine and said, "Hello William, have you come along to help us at last?"

Surprised at finding someone that he had known for around twenty years as soon as he arrived on the site, William quickly retorted, "No I've come down to see who was making all that bloody noise! I should have known that it would be you!"

Harry, the driver of the loco, replied, "I've got a couple of minutes for a 'brew up' – fancy a cuppa?"

As soon as William indicated that a cuppa would be very welcome he was invited onto the footplate.

Sitting quietly drinking their tea while the fireman ran the pricker around the firebox, William looked at the rake of carriages behind the engine and asked, "Where did this lot come from?"

Harry replied, "We've had to draw them in off the main line, because the NUR* is threatening to 'black' all movements onto the branch from the main line"

"But how did you get hold of them?" asked William.

"We bought them," replied Harry.

"How the hell did you manage to get the money?" asked William, astonished.

"By persuading anyone that we could find to sell raffle tickets at 5p a time," was the answer.

William still remained doubtful.

"But what's the point of purchasing carriages, and wagons when you're not going to be able to open the line for some considerable time?" he asked.

Pausing only to light up his cigarette Harry said, "The Public Inquiry has finished, and we are confident that we are going to be allowed to reopen the line. As soon as the decision is announced we will arrange for the Railway Inspector to check the section of line between Minehead and Blue Anchor, and as soon as we have got his approval, we can open for business."

At last William was beginning to be affected by Harry's enthusiasm, and he asked, "Well, if I did come along, what could I do?"

Harry looked at him in amusement, then said, "You are an experienced fitter on steam locos, but most of that work is being carried out at Minehead. You are also a qualified diesel fitter and we've got a couple of DMU sets up here that need attention. I understand that you're a handy carpenter: there's a lot of refurbishment work to be undertaken on these coaches before they can enter service, and some replacement planks have got to be fitted to the goods wagons before we can use them on the permanent way trains. How's that for starters then? When you finish that lot we can probably find you some other jobs to do."

Before climbing down from the cab of the loco William promised to think about Harry's suggestion.

"I'm here every day, you can always come down for a chat, even if you decide that you are too old to do anything useful," Harry informed William.

As soon as he walked through the door Nadine started to question him about what he had seen, what was happening, and if he still want to get involved.

"Please woman, let me eat my meal, and gather my thoughts together, then I will tell you all that has happened, as soon as I have finished the washing up."

As they sat down with their cup of tea after the chores were completed, Nadine's first word was, "Well?"

William then started to tell his wife of the events that had unfolded during his visit to the station that morning, of his meeting with Harry, the engines and rolling stock that had been acquired, the volunteers' hopes, and the management's plans for the future.

No sooner had he finished his explanation, than Nadine asked, "Well, what have you decided to do? Do you still want to be involved?"

Looking at the floor, William muttered, "I don't want to go out and leave you on your own."

Nadine realised that what he meant was, yes, he did want to be involved, but at the same time did not want to risk annoying or upsetting her by going back on his word.

She had listened carefully to what he had been saying, and had made up her mind what she wanted to do long before he had finished recounting his experiences of that morning. So she promptly replied, "They want people to work on sales stands, to sell raffle tickets, and serve cups of tea in the shop they are hoping to open: I can do all of those tasks. If I undertake them, I would be releasing men to do the heavier work that needs to be done. So when are you thinking of going down to see Harry then?"

William thought for some time and then said, "I must complete some of the benches that have been ordered before I get involved down there: I can't let those people down who have been kind enough to give me orders, so I think that I will leave it for a while."

He then continued, "Also, the prospect of working out in the open air servicing DMUs or steam locos in the pouring rain, and the cold, worries me, because when I work in the cold and the wet, my back starts to play up."

As this was the first time that William had complained about his back, Nadine assumed that this was another excuse by him to delay the time before he had to make a decision.

She knew that if she allowed William to continue to put off until tomorrow, what he should be doing today, he would never get involved, and eventually he would regret his decision.

"That means that if you don't go down there, I can't become involved either," Nadine replied. "You don't have to work out in the open. They have practically asked you to work on the refurbishment of the carriages and if you do that you can work inside the coaches when the weather is bad, so you won't risk hurting your back."

"What about the benches I've got to build?" asked William, weakening.

"Why don't you tell Harry that to start with you can help them for two days a week, and then you can work on your benches for the remainder of the week," Nadine suggested.

From past experience William knew that before long, emergencies would occur and there was every possibility that he would be asked to work a third day each week, then a fourth, until in the end he would be working seven days a week on the railway. He also knew that if he voiced these fears to Nadine, she would either inform him that he was being negative, or that it was up to him to say no! Realising that there was no point in arguing with his wife, he informed her that he would walk down to the station the next day and see Harry to sort something out.

"Good," said Nadine. "Then I can come down with you and find a job that I can do."

As a result of his visit the following morning William soon found himself working two days a week, Wednesdays and Thursdays, on the six Mk1 coaches that the fledgling company had acquired. Nadine found herself selling raffle tickets, and helping out on the sales stand, mainly at weekends, and often at Minehead station. When Nadine was rostered for duty at the other end of the line William would drive her down to Minehead, and then wait for her until she had finished. While he was waiting for her one day, he strolled into the former goods shed, and when he heard a torrent of bad language coming from behind a Bagnall locomotive inside the building, he strolled over to see what was happening.

He found that two fitters had been attempting to replace a coupling rod on the engine, and it had slipped and landed on the foot of one of them, and that was the reason for the bad language. It was obvious that the man was in considerable pain, but he was attempting to carry on because it was essential that the work be completed that night. After arranging for someone to drive the injured man to the local hospital for an X ray, William rolled up his sleeves, and helped the second fitter to complete the job. Although neither Nadine nor William realised it at the time, this was to be the first of many occasions that she would have to wait for William, while he worked on yet another emergency in the locomotive shed at Minehead.

A shortly time later, the volunteers heard the news that they had all been waiting for. In spite of the objections of the Western National bus company, the NUR, and the residents of some second homes in the area, the inquiry had found in their favour. Finally, on Tuesday 23rd March 1976, Major Peter Olver for the Railway Inspectorate carried out his inspection, and cleared the line for use by passenger trains. This was the moment that the volunteers had been preparing for, and they redoubled their efforts to ensure that everything would be ship-shape, and spick and span, and would run smoothly when the line re-opened on the following Sunday 28th March.

That day, Nadine and William like many thousands of others, drove to Minehead, arriving there long before 10am when the re-opening ceremony was due to be performed by Lord Montagu of Beaulieu. There was a bitterly cold wind blowing that day, and it was also threatening to rain, but both Nadine and William, with the other volunteers who were present that day, felt a warm glow as they watched an immaculate, and highly polished 'Victor', complete with bunting, slowly back down the track alongside the platform, and couple up to the six carriages waiting there.

After the band finished playing, and the speeches had been given, the first train was flagged away by Lord Montagu on its short journey. Later that day Nadine and William along with two thousand other passengers travelled on one of the numerous trips the train made to Blue Anchor. That evening as they returned home by car, they both found themselves wondering how long it would be before they could make that same journey to Bishops Lydeard by rail again. On the 23rd August that same year the volunteers succeeded in re-opening the line as far as Williton.

Many volunteers, together with the all too few members of the paid staff, undertook the numerous tasks involved in maintaining the services to and from Minehead and Williton, and others continued with the task of clearing and restoring the next sections of the track. William and Nadine worked on the many jobs that had to be undertaken at Bishops Lydeard before the whole length of the line could be re-opened. William worked with others on the task of converting a siphon wagon into a sales coach. Later he helped convert a Mark 1 coach into a sales shop, and the original shop was then adapted to serve tea and coffee to the visitors who came to the station. Nadine found herself helping out in both the shop and the cafeteria.

The number of days that William worked on the railway varied from week to week, depending on the project that he was working on, and the degree of urgency that was needed to complete it. He also continued to build his garden seats. One day he was asked to build a garden table, and before long he was receiving a steady stream of orders for these, and bird feeders, nesting boxes, and even pergolas. As he was later to remark his hobby had become a steady little earner.

Working at Bishops Lydeard neither Nadine nor William was directly involved in many of the crises that were to trouble the new company before the line was reopened to Bishops Lydeard, although they, with everyone else working on the line, spent many anxious hours, and days, wondering if the company would survive the latest financial problem.

When the trains did eventually reach Bishops Lydeard on the 9th June 1979, both Nadine and William were working on the station that day. Nadine was working in the old booking office on platform one, selling tickets to intending passengers, and found herself rushed off her feet all day. By contrast, William had a more leisurely time, together with a grandstand view of all the proceedings, as he made the signal box at the end of platform two weatherproof. He also replaced the floorboards and the outside steps in preparation for the time when a new frame and all the locking gear would be installed.

As everyone involved on the WSR had come to expect by now, the day did not pass without the customary crisis. The previous evening Victor, one of the two Bagnall locomotives in use on the line had been failed at Minehead with blown boiler tubes, and despite the efforts of the fitters who worked on the loco all night, it was not ready for service the following morning. Fortunately, once again the Diesel & Electric Group based at Williton were able to provide a diesel locomotive to haul the first train out of Minehead bound for Bishops Lydeard that day.

It was also fortunate that the other Bagnall, Vulcan, behaved perfectly and it was sent on its way by Mr Ulick Huntington, the chairman of the Parish Council. The elation of the onlookers at seeing the first train from Bishops Lydeard pull out of the station on time, with two hundred passengers on board, quickly turned to concern when they saw the train come to a standstill only two hundred and fifty yards from the station at the start its long climb up the bank towards Crowcombe station. The driver of the engine then gave several long blasts on the loco's whistle, and they saw the fireman climb down from the cab of the engine and walk round to the front of it.

After what seemed a lifetime to the onlookers, but in reality was only a minute or so, the fireman re-appeared and after he had climbed back on board the engine, the driver gave another blast on the loco's whistle, and the train started to pull slowly away. Later the onlookers were to learn that the problem had been caused by two dogs who had decided to take their customary nap in the middle of the 'Four foot', and because they had been indulging in the practice for some time past, saw no reason why their nap should be disturbed simply because a train appeared.

Together with the other volunteers and the paid staff working on the WSR William and Nadine had hoped that once the whole line was reopened as far as Bishops Lydeard, the problems that had beset the line since it re-opened would ease. Unfortunately this was not to be, and for a number of years the line seemed to stagger from one financial crisis to another.

It was to be eight years after trains started to run to Bishops Lydeard before the company could install a water tank and replenish the tanks on the steam engines when they arrived from Minehead. That same year a locomotive powerful enough to pull an eight-coach train along the entire length of the line became available. When the restoration of a second former main line locomotive was completed the following year, passengers were at last able to travel over the entire length of the line by a steam train, instead changing to and from diesel trains at Williton as they had done in the past.

During this period, William continued be involved on numerous projects on the railway, including working with others on the set of coaches fitted out for the Quantock Belle luxury dining train, and numerous small projects like platform seats, sack trucks, and luggage barrows. From time to time his help was sought when one of the DMUs that operated the shuttle service to Williton became temperamental, and his expertise as a diesel fitter was sought. It was during this period that Nadine's skill as a cook was often in demand for the dining services provided on the Quantock Belle.

In 1989 William was eighty years old and Nadine was sixty-nine. He was still obtaining a few orders to build garden furniture, and the railway at last seemed to be prospering. That year the railway succeeded in attracting far more visitors than ever before, and as more people became aware of the potential of the railway, the number of volunteers available to assist with the numerous projects started to increase. This was just as well because as funds became available, many more projects were planned.

One sunny summer Sunday morning that year, William was standing on the end of the platform at Bishops Lydeard being jostled by many visitors who, like him, were waiting to get a glimpse of 'Evening Star' as it arrived with an eight coach train packed with passengers from Minehead. Suddenly William found himself wondering what his grandfather would have made of it all: the closure of the line, the re-opening, the huge crowds waiting to travel on the trains – probably more people on the platform in one day than Jon would have seen using the station in a whole year. The big engines that were using the branch line were also far larger than any that travelled along it in former days.

After the return train had departed, taking with it many of the passengers who had been crowded on the platform, William remained seated on a platform seat in the warm sunshine talking to David, the stationmaster.

"Do you know," he mused, "I've been looking at all this activity today, wondering what my grandfather would have made of all the changes that have taken place recently, if he had still been alive."

He was astonished when David replied, "He would be even more surprised if he were to come back in two, or three year's time. By then we hope that the signal box will be operating, the platform will have been extended, a bay platform built, the old booking office will have been closed, and a new one built on platform two, and the existing carriage which serves as a shop, will have been replaced by a custom - built building!"

After thinking over what he had been told for a while, William replied, "If that is the case, I think that perhaps I am getting to be too old to be involved in projects of that size! Now that you are getting all these new volunteers coming along perhaps it is time for me to hang up my overalls: I don't think I could cope with that lot!"

David replied, "I can understand how you feel, but would you be prepared to help in an advisory capacity, by planning the sequence in which the various tasks should be carried out, supervising, and checking that the work had been carried out satisfactorily?"

William agreed to think the matter over, and strolled slowly back to his home for the Sunday lunch that Nadine had prepared. When they were both sitting down with their afternoon cup of teas, after finishing their lunch and doing the washing up, William told Nadine of his conversation with David that morning. Although he had been uncertain what reply he was likely to get from his wife, he certainly did not expect to hear her say, "We both seem to have forgotten that we retired so that we could spend more time with each other, and now very often we only seem to see each other when we are going to bed or having breakfast in the morning. Please don't look so downcast William, it is as much my fault as yours! But I do feel that now the railway is on its feet and more people are coming forward to help, perhaps we should start to spend more time with each other before it is too late."

William's response to this observation was a long, "Mmmmmmm."

Knowing what was going through her husband's mind Nadine continued, "I don't want you to give up going down to the railway altogether, but I do want you to take things a little easier, before you make yourself ill. So why don't you ask David what he had in mind and how many days a week he would expect you to go down there. I can't give up the railway completely either, but in future I shall be serving teas on one day a week in the new shop when it opens."

Having received an assurance from David that his services would only be required on an irregular basis, and certainly not for more than one day a week at the most, William saw all the projects they had discussed that Sunday morning come to fruition during the next decade, although during that time Nadine decided that she could no longer play an active part on the railway herself.

By the start of the twenty-first century, William was finding the walk to the station becoming very difficult for him to undertake, and whenever he wanted to visit his old friends he was collected from his home by a volunteer and driven in a car to the station. On one particular occasion he arrived to find that the floor of the old booking office, which had been used as a mess room after the new booking office had been built, was being replaced. To achieve this all the furniture in the room, most of which had been fixed to the walls, was being carefully released, so that it could be stored and re-instated in the office once the floor had been replaced. When they detached the old stationmaster's desk from the position it had occupied for nearly 140 years, there was a rustling sound as some papers, which had been trapped behind the desk for many years, fell to the floor.

One of the volunteers quickly retrieved the document, and then realised that it was the former stationmaster's log book covering the period from the 1860s through to the 1920s. Carefully turning the pages that were by now so brittle that as he attempted to turn them they started to break up, the finder who had become absorbed in the document, suddenly turned to William and said, "Hey, William, there's a chap in here called Jon Hawkes – was he related to you in any way?"

Crossing the office as quickly as he could, tears welled in William's eyes when he saw the once familiar copperplate handwriting that he had last seen in the signalman's logbook that his grandfather had kept in the nearby signal box ninety years earlier.

234

FOOTNOTE

It was decided by the West Somerset Railway Association that because this document was of such historical interest an attempt should be made to preserve it, and bring its contents to the attention of a much wider audience. To achieve these aims, and in an attempt to recover some of the costs incurred in impregnating the logbook with silicone to preserve it, a booklet was written entitled, 'Good Times - Bad Times', which gave a fictional account of the life of William's grandfather. Copies of the new edition of this book, published in 2005, are available from retail outlets on the W.S.R. and other shops in the West Somerset Area.

William died in his sleep before the booklet was published, and it was only as she read the book after William's death that Nadine realised just how alike her husband and his grandfather had been, and from where William had got his passion for railways.

GLOSSARY

Page:

7   **anti-macassars**: macassar oil was used as hair oil, so an anti-macassar kept the oil from marking the back of a chair.

8   **copper**: a metal tub in a bricked enclosure with a small grate underneath, normally found in the corner of the kitchen or outhouse. The cold water was poured into the tub by means of buckets, and the fire lit in a grate underneath to heat the water, so that all the washing could be boiled. It was also used at Christmas to boil Christmas puddings and on washdays to boil other delicacies like spotted dick, etc.

9   **mangle**: a device with two large wooden rollers which were turned by means of a handle at the side, through which the clean washing was passed to wring out the surplus water before the clothes were hung out on the line to dry.

16   **brilliantined**: brilliantine was a perfumed hair oil, making hair glossy.

19   **GWR**: Great Western Railway

27   **comptometer**: a very early form of mechanical desktop calculator. It was rather bulky by modern standards and was normally housed on a low desk that was at a right angle to the operator's main desk on which all the paperwork was placed. All calculations were in pounds sterling, with buttons on them for pounds (single, tens, hundreds, and thousands), shillings (ten and individual shillings), and pence (up to 11) with additional buttons for farthings, halfpennies, and three farthings. Once the keys had been pressed for the requisite number of times the answer appeared in individual windows for each column at the front of the machine.

236

30   **dictaphone**: the very early version of the modern tape recorder. The letter was dictated by means of a horn onto a revolving wax cylinder. When the letter had been dictated the cylinder was removed and given to the typist, who then fitted it into another machine to be played back using another horn to enable her to listen to the message, or later through a set of earphones.

76   *schmutter:* Jewish expression for clothing, rag

85   **Brylcreemed**: Brylcreem was a cream used by men for hair styling.

107   WRAC; WRNS; WAAF: Women's Royal Army Corps; Women's Royal Navy Service; Women's Auxiliary Air Force

115   **WVS**: Women's Voluntary Service.

115   **public slipper baths**: partially covered, slipper-shaped baths, available for hire at public baths.

122   **American PX unit**: a shop selling goods for US servicemen overseas (from Post Exchange).

122   **NAAFI**: organisation providing canteens for servicemen (from Navy, Army and Air Force Institute).

123   **USATC**: the United States Army Transportation Corps

131   **British Restaurant**: where the public could buy a nutritious meal for one shilling without using their food ration points.

136   **V1**: German bomb, also called a doodle bug: when their noise stopped, they fell.

140   **V2**: later model of German bomb, the first long range ballistic missile.

146   **iron rations**: ration of concentrated food for an extreme emergency.

166   **S&D Station**: Somerset and Dorset Railway Station.

167   **DBST**: Double British Summer Time (to save electricity)

172   **pre-fab bungalows**: pre-fabricated, cheap and easy to erect, designed to be temporary.

183   **ATS**: Auxiliary Territorial Service (replaced by WRAC in 1949).

222   **NUR**: National Union of Railwaymen.

FACT FILE

At the height of the Blitz an estimated 200,000 Londoners took shelter in underground stations.

In the four months leading up to New Year's Eve 1940, more than 13,000 people were killed by enemy bombing in London.

Rationing was introduced in January 1940:
Butter, sugar, ham and bacon were the first commodities to be restricted.
By 1944 one week's food ration for an adult included:
     8 ounces (230 grams) of sugar;
     2½ pints (1.4 litres) of milk;
     2½ ounces (70 grams) of tea;
     3 ounces (85 grams) of beans;
     4 ounces (110 grams) of butter;
     2 ounces (55 grams) of cheese;
     2 ounces (55 grams) of margarine;
     4 ounces (110 grams) of bacon;
     3 ounces (85 grams) of sweets;
The meat ration was one shilling (5p) worth of 'carcass meat' and two pence (½p) of tinned meat.
Each person was allowed 31 eggs per year.

Every morning after the 8am news on the Home Service the Ministry of Food put out a five minute programme in which the radio doctor dispensed tips on how to keep fit and healthy on the food available.

Potato consumption increased by 60% during the war.

Each person's clothing allowance was 66 coupons per year:
    A long-sleeved dress took 11 coupons;
    a jacket 13 coupons;
    a raincoat 9 coupons.

The average man's earnings were £4 13s (£4.65) per week.

Cigarettes cost 2½d (1p) for a packet of five.

A lipstick cost 6d (2.5p).

Postage stamps cost 2½d (1p) for civilians. Letters home from the French front were ½d.

The most popular car was an 8 horse power Ford 8, which cost £300.